JEFFERSON COUNTY LIBRARY
620 Cedar Avenue
Port Hadlock, WA 98339
(360) 385-6544   www.jclibrary.info

ABOUT A
MOUNTAIN

ABOUT A
MOUNTAIN

JOHN D'AGATA

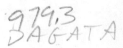

W. W. NORTON & COMPANY

NEW YORK • LONDON

For information about permission to reproduce selections from this book,
write to Permissions, W. W. Norton & Company, Inc.,
500 Fifth Avenue, New York, NY 10110

For information about special discounts for bulk purchases, please contact
W. W. Norton Special Sales at specialsales@wwnorton.com or 800-233-4830

Manufacturing by Courier Westford
Book design by Chris Welch
Production manager: Anna Oler

Library of Congress Cataloging-in-Publication Data

D'Agata, John, 1974–

About a mountain / John D'Agata.

p. cm.

Includes bibliographical references.

ISBN 978-0-393-06818-4 (hardcover)

1. Radioactive waste repositories—Nevada—Yucca Mountain.
2. Las Vegas Metropolitain Area (Nev.)—Social life and customs.
3. Yucca Mountain (Nev.) I. Title.

TD898.12.N3D335 2010

979.3'13503—dc22

2009039295

W. W. Norton & Company, Inc.
500 Fifth Avenue, New York, N.Y. 10110
www.wwnorton.com

W. W. Norton & Company Ltd.
Castle House, 75/76 Wells Street, London W1T 3QT

1 2 3 4 5 6 7 8 9 0

To whomever I did not help.

It seemed to us that we were a very great people.

—THE UNITED STATES OF AMERICA

WHO

If you take the population of Las Vegas, Nevada, and you divide that by the number of days in the year, there should be 5,000 people in the city and its suburbs with a birthday on the same day that Las Vegas began.

On the hundredth anniversary of its founding, however, Las Vegas had only gathered twenty-nine of those people.

One of them arrived in a beaded blue headdress, her eyelashes sequined, her ruffled skirt torn.

Another stood smiling as he watched her while she preened.

There was a child in a knapsack. Its mother on the phone.

An Elvis showed up briefly. Turned out that he was lost.

A small family arrived carrying posters of their daughter: *1979–2005 . . . IT WOULD BE HER BIRTHDAY TOO!*

All of us were there awaiting guidance from the city, assembled in a downtown fast food parking lot, seven thirty in the morning, the beginning of the summer.

This was May 15. And I had just turned thirty.

"You of all people," wrote the city in a letter, "know how special our city really is . . . [because] Las Vegas is literally in your blood! Won't you help us celebrate your bond with Las Vegas by marching in this summer's Centennial Parade?"

When a city official arrived, we were told what we should do.

"Smile! . . . Be psyched! . . . This party is for you!"

My mom was there to wait with me, but they asked if she would march.

"When's your birthday, by the way?"

"Late July," said my mom.

"Close enough," she was told.

We were positioned behind the mayor, and he behind six horses, and they behind the color guard from Nellis Air Force Base.

A young man with a shovel and a wheelbarrow marched beside us, stopping every now and then to scrape up the horses' shit.

"I'm from Atlanta," said the guy who marched beside my mom and me. "But me and my wife come out here once or twice a year to play. Guess that's why they asked me. I don't care, right? I'll march in their motherfucker."

We marched past Kostner's Cash, and we marched past Super Cash, and we marched past Gambler's Pawn and Loan, and then an empty lot.

Past Drive-Up Wedding, Bail Bonds Now, *45% OFF ALL OUR LADIES' STOLES AND FURS*.

We marched into an area that locals call the Naked City, a neighborhood once inhabited by the city's many show-girls, and then by many vagrants, and now by seven signs for Adopt-A-Block Las Vegas.

SMILE! blinked a monitor as we neared some TV crews.

YOU ARE NOW ENTERING A LIVE TELEVISION PERFORMANCE AREA!

SMILE!

SMILE!

SMILE!

SMILE!

"What do you want to say to America today?" asked a woman in a pantsuit while gripping a microphone, beside her a man in tight blue jeans, an open shirt, a ponytail, a camera on his shoulder with its black cord twisting up the street into a van.

"This is wild!" yelled the man who marched beside my mom and me. "Happy Birthday, Vegas, yo! I love you all, Atlanta!"

We passed the bank of cameras and waved the posters we were given. Twirled some streamers, tossed confetti, shot compression-powered string. We stood and sang the birthday song to a grandstand in applause.

"You guys rock!" yelled a woman from the grandstand as we passed. And then we reached the end of the grandstand, and were done.

We turned around, joined the crowd, watched the others march.

The Sons of Norway's Viking ship rocked sideways on its chassis.

The public library's Book Drill Team passed out their branches' hours.

Seven Chinese boys held aloft an orange dragon.

There were women marching silently behind a plastic banner: *1-800-BETS-OFF . . . CALL IF YOU NEED HELP!*

Men who drove old cars.

Girls with 4-H calves.

Old women wearing pageant crowns.

Congressmen, dairy carts, ballroom dancers, Meadows Chevy, the Organization of Ladies Kazoo Post-92 from Laughlin—over two hundred different entries marching past us for three hours.

All of them being applauded, waved at, snapshot.

Broadcast on the news, on local public access, on videophone recordings that were posted to the Web.

The parade was called by one newscast "the happening of the century!"

A local blogger wrote that "something special happened here!"

A radio host asked listeners if "all that really happened?"

And the mayor swore that this parade was going to be remembered "as one of the greatest things to ever happen in Las Vegas."

And while I wasn't born there, and have since then moved away, during the summer I lived in Vegas I began to feel those claims, appealing in their hopefulness the way parades appeal, the way a list appeals to those with faith in withheld meanings: the dream that if we linger long enough with anything, the truth of its significance is bound to be revealed.

WHAT

When I helped my mother move to Las Vegas that May, we lived for a couple weeks at the Budget Suites of America, a low-rise concrete pink motel with AIR COND and WEEKLY RATES and a Burger King next door.

We started to look for houses in developments called "Provence," "Tuscany," and "Bridgeport Landing," wandering through their model homes on plastic carpet runners.

In the master bedroom suites there were books displayed on beds, their dust jackets removed, their spines always up, their titles too faint to clearly read at a glance.

In the mud rooms there were chalkboards with the reminder, *Buy milk!* Mason jars of pasta in the kitchens neatly spilled. Ceramic white bowls for family pets on the floor. Silk flowers in blue vases on the dining room tables sparkling with little specks of round plastic morning dew.

There were terra-cotta tiles.

There were screened-in lanais.

There were entertainment centers in every living room.

The model called the "Amador" had columns beside its door. The "Palomar" had room for four cars in its garage. And "Versailles," gleaming white, came with an optional motorized gate.

In every house the smell of cookies wafted golden brown from a stainless-steel oven that hadn't been plugged in.

"All you have to do," said one hostess in a house, "is pick your model and your lot, and then leave the rest to us!"

During one of those summer mornings upon first moving there, my mother and I stood in the sand of Las Vegas, listening to a broker around some wooden stakes and flags, some white-chalked land plots and orange-painted pipes, trying to see what he was seeing as he motioned with his hands, as he motioned with his wrists and wriggly fingers in full circles, motioned before his face, above his head, and to my mom, motioned toward the west, and then to me, and off the lot, then motioned past the stakes, the whipping flags, the lines in sand, beyond to where some pocks of little yucca plants were blooming, their tiny white flowers that never open all the way, their wobbly tall stalks of puffy million-seeded pods, their sword-long fronds that always indicate a desert, fanning out beyond the yellow of the lot in which we stood, fanning north above the shadow cast down by a mountain, fanning up and fanning over, fanning down and fanning out, then fanning off the private acreage that defines Summerlin, the walled and gated community my mother came to live in: orange houses, green parks, a white clocktower at its heart.

"You gotta imagine the land out here without all these weeds and stuff," the broker told my mother as he kicked a yucca plant. "You're on your back lawn, easy tunes, iced tea. Maybe a little water feature bubbling in the distance."

We stood there on a $100,000 one-eighth-acre lot because Ethan, my mother's broker, had said that living in this community would be like living in New England, my mother's home for the previous sixty-seven years.

"I like to tell people," Ethan told us, "that more trees line the sidewalks of Summerlin per capita than any other neighborhood here in Las Vegas." It was a fact he seemed particularly sure of as he shared it because, according to Ethan, the builder of Summerlin had surveyed the number of trees in the neighborhoods of other builders, divided that by the number of residents in each, then ordered 15 percent more trees than the highest of those estimates.

In the Spanish, we learned, *las vegas* means "the meadows," a lush haven that was named in 1829 for the "miles of green peace" it offered early pioneers. That first Spanish scout who wandered into Las Vegas said that it appeared "like a godsend" to him, "a great lie within the desert," "unbelievable," "unexpected," "surely the truest proof that this land is touched by God."

We walked through the sand, onto sidewalk again, up the two steps into Ethan's red Chevy S-10, then drove across the yellow lots of yucca-dotted desert, past gray concrete walls that were still being stacked, then finished concrete walls being painted further in, beige concrete walls keeping yuccas off of lawns, beige concrete walls lined with saplings, lamps, and shrubs, beige concrete walls with red swing-set tops behind them.

"This was all green at one point, as far as the eye can see. Meadows . . . meadows . . . green meadows," Ethan said. "That's what Summerlin's all about, bringing all that nature back."

Now, in Las Vegas, there is a Country Club at the Meadows, a Golden Meadows Nursing Home, Meadows Coffee, Meadows Jewelry, Meadows Mortgage, Meadows Glass, Meadows Hospital, Automotive, Alterations, and Pets. The Meadows Country Day School is a private K through six. Meadows Women's Center is in Village Meadows Mall. Meadows Trailer Park has a waiting list for lots. And the Meadows Church of Light has a Christ on its marquee.

Barefoot, white-ankled, he's teaching in a meadow.

When Summerlin was started in 1988, its developer said that it wanted to create "the most successful master planned community in America," and as we entered the town's center, called The Town Center at Summerlin, Ethan explained that the goal of the builder had already been surpassed, even with only two thirds of the development complete.

"Someone moves into a new Summerlin home every two hours and twenty-two minutes," he said.

We circled in The Town Center at Summerlin's parking lot, idled behind a Lexus, beside a fountain, under sun. Then Ethan led us deeper into the center of the town, past Jamba Juice and Quiznos and Starbucks storefronts, past the life-sized bronze statues of a shopping mom and son, and into a green expanse called Willow Park at Summerlin, a three-acre fluffy stretch of shrubs and white flowers and a long mattress lawn toward which Ethan spread his arms.

"This is what living in Summerlin is all about," he said.

Acrobats in sequined shorts flipped backward down the lawn. A mime followed behind a man who licked an ice cream cone. A stilt-walker, burger stand, barbershop quartet. Children chased each other with their faces brightly painted. Dogs chased the children with their eyes as they heeled. Above the park on two white poles two banners stretched and waved:

SUMMERLIN NUMBER ONE!

and

GUINNESS BOOK OF RECORDS WORLD'S LARGEST GROUP HUG!

"Okay," Ethan said, "I'll be honest with ya, right? It won't be like this every day that you're living in Las Vegas. But I just wanted to show you how much spirit we all have! You can tell that everyone's really psyched to be living here, right?"

Of the 335,000 acres that constitute the valley Las Vegas

occupies, only 49,000 remain undeveloped. According to the Nevada Development Authority's annual brochure, *Las Vegas Perspective*, 8,500 people move into the city every single month. It is the fastest growing metropolitan area in America. As a result, the Las Vegas valley's shortage of land has become so pronounced that a local paper once reported that two new acres of land in Las Vegas are developed every hour, on each of which are squeezed an average of eight three-bedroom homes.

Indeed, even as early as 1962, when the population of Las Vegas was one thirtieth its current size, the natural springs that fed the city's growing population began to noticeably dry, and then to be depleted, and then to sink forever beneath the reach of Las Vegas.

The city built a pipeline through the desert, therefore, running fifty miles into the city from Lake Mead, the artificial lake that was formed by Hoover Dam, the largest artificial body of water in the world. Today, the pipeline carries 97 percent of all the water Las Vegas uses, although the lake that it's been tapping for over fifty-five years is now ninety feet below what it normally should be, 58 percent of its usual capacity, losing about a trillion gallons of water every year.

According to the Scripps Institution of Oceanography, there's a 50 percent chance that within a dozen years the lake will be completely dry.

During that summer when my mom and I arrived, the lake's surface reached what was being called by locals "a potentially low level," but which hydrologists from everywhere else were starting to call "an absolute ecological disaster," something symptomatic of "a cataclysmic drought" or "the worst drought in a century" or "the worst drought in North America in over 500 years" or:

> "I'm not even sure this actually qualifies as a 'drought'. This really might be closer to what this valley's naturally like: dry and brown and no place for human beings. . . . What we know is that over two centuries ago an extraordinary cycle of rainfall was just beginning in the valley. And as would be expected, such unusual increases in precipitation brought with them the appearance of 'meadows' in this valley, shallow-rooted shrubbery that are usually indicative of something aberrant going on . . . at least when it comes to a desert . . . [for] what should be in Las Vegas is sagebrush and creosote and hundreds of thousands of yuccas. But Las Vegas isn't the kind of place that takes 'no' for an answer. The city wanted to exist. The city got what it asked for."

Indeed, as warnings of a drought proliferated that summer, the general manager of the Las Vegas Water Authority said that "the notion that we have only a finite amount of water, and that when that water is gone we'll have to stop our city's growth, is a notion that belongs in the distant past."

And so, we settled in.

We moved my mother's cat, her books, her pinball machine, the three floors and five bedrooms of boxes from home. We planted a tomato in a large pot outside, bought green plastic chairs and a table for the deck, hung drapes to frame the view of the fairway in the back, the green promise we couldn't play on but paid extra to live beside, and took a trip to see the lake that had made that promise possible, the blue shock in yellow rock that attracts more campers and boaters and fishers and swimmers and skiers and hikers and divers and Scouts than any other National Recreation Area—7 million annual visitors on average—an estimate that the National Park Service raised to 8 million visitors by the end of that summer, an increase which one ranger tried to explain was not caused by more campers or boaters or fishers or swimmers or skiers or hikers or Scouts, but by amateur archeologists, owners of metal detectors, history buffs, photographers, and those who used to live there. For what attracted the extra million visitors to Lake Mead that year was not the usual lure of the lake's artificial beauty, nor its recreational usefulness, nor even just the novelty that such a lake could exist, but rather the simple fact that the lake was slowly dying, that as the city quickly drained it the lake's level lowered, and there slowly reemerged from its sinking blue surface that far distant past of the city of Las Vegas: a chimney stack from a concrete plant poking higher and higher above the water every day, part of a giant complex of mixing vats and grinders that was built in the thirties to help pour Hoover Dam, then was flooded by the lake that the dam had helped form; there was the B-29 bomber that crashed into Lake Mead, left there by the Air Force in 1949 because at that time it was so deep that divers couldn't reach it; there was the sundae shop; there was the baker's shop; there was the grocery store; a bank; there were 233 crypts and tombstones that were stripped bare of clothing and necklaces and bones when every deceased resident of St. Thomas, Nevada, was ziplocked and carted north and reburied upriver, just days before the growing lake would swallow their town whole.

Even a 5,000-year-old city reemerged, the ancient Indian settlement called the "Anasazi Lost City," a name it didn't receive because the city had been misplaced, but rather because the city, up until that dry summer, had remained one of the country's only pre-Columbian listings to be catalogued as "submerged" on the National Register of Historic Places.

"We may not have a history that's as deep as other cities," said a megaphoned voice in Summerlin that day, "and we may not be the biggest in America yet, but ladies and gentlemen do you know what we are?"

What? yelled the park.

"We are the city of big spirit!"

Some dogs barked, the park clapped, Ethan cheered and then he *woo*ed. It was noon and a stilt-walker's legs were on the ground, heat was sweating lines down the faces of some clowns, dogs were lapping ice cream off the bushes in the park, and the megaphoned voice said: "All right, now, let's go!"

Las Vegas was a city, it was suggested that morning, that often came together in community spirit. After all, it had come together in order to watch the old Dunes Hotel be imploded to make way for the lake outside Bellagio. It had

come together in order to watch the Landmark, the Alad-
din, the Sands, the Hacienda, and the Desert Inn hotels be
imploded as well. And it would come together later, in the
culmination of the city's centennial celebrations, in order to
watch the implosion of the Stardust Hotel, the oldest remaining casino on the Las Vegas Strip, an event that attracted three
TV news copters, two dozen articles in local newspapers,
special rates for hotel rooms overlooking the implosion, a six-
course Implosion Dinner-for-Two, and 19,462 more people
than the 538 Summerlin neighbors who convened that sunny
morning in a green bushy park in order to prove that Vegas
had community spirit, an effort that they made on behalf of
the city, but without the news copters or the dinners-for-two
or the 363 extra group huggers that they needed to unseat
the current record-holding huggers, the 900 employees of
Goldman Sachs in New York.

WHEN

I hadn't planned to stay.

What I'd planned to do was help my mother find her new home. Help her move in. Get my mom settled.

But within a couple weeks she took up with a local group of environmental activists, meeting them every other week at a bar near her home called Viva Lost Wages, where they liked to watch C-SPAN.

I went with her one week to an unscheduled meeting because an e-mail message in boldfaced caps proclaimed the meeting *"ESSENTIAL IF YOU LOVE LIVING IN LAS VEGAS!"*

"We are going to watch someone single-handedly save our city," said the leader of my mom's group when she and I arrived.

I looked over and up at C-SPAN.

The bartender raised the volume on the TV to max.

There at a podium above the Lost Wages jukebox was the senior senator from Nevada, Democrat Harry Reid.

"What we are talking about today," said Democrat Harry Reid, "is the single greatest threat to the future of our nation."

"You give 'em hell, Harry!" said the bartender.

Someone else said, "Yeah!"

I only knew a little about Harry Reid at that point. I knew that he had just been named by a local weekly paper "Our Favorite Politician in the State of Nevada," due to what that weekly called his "consistent and quiet decency." I had also seen Reid at an oil change shop staring hard from the cover of *Las Vegas Life* magazine, recently having been named "The Most Powerful Man in Our City" because of his "bold willingness to compromise for results." And even my mom, who seldom trusts anyone, came home from her first meeting with the environmental group to tell me that Harry Reid was "the best hope this city has to stop Yucca Mountain."

What's Yucca Mountain? I asked.

"Watch," someone said.

"Ever since I was elected to Congress," Reid told his constituents earlier that summer, "I have been fighting against Yucca Mountain because it threatens the health and security of everyone in our state. The science they're doing there is incomplete, faulty, and totally unsafe. Yucca Mountain is the worst place in America to store nuclear waste, and that's why I'm committed to making sure it never happens."

The idea to store nuclear waste inside Yucca Mountain had originated approximately thirty years earlier, during the height of American protests against nuclear energy. To try to change public opinion about nuclear power, the American Nuclear Energy Council, the lobbying organization for the nuclear power industry, suggested to its clients that Americans would be less afraid of nuclear power plants if they could be assured that nuclear waste was being safely stored.

"This," said the council, "is what Americans are afraid of . . . [it's] not the power that we produce."

So in 1980, one year after a nuclear plant overheated at Three Mile Island, the American Nuclear Energy Council began to lobby Congress for legislation that would require that the nuclear waste produced at its clients' power plants be stored by the federal government at a single national site.

"Of course, there's no direct correlation between the dangers that are posed by nuclear waste and those by a nuclear meltdown," the leader of my mom's group explained to us at Viva. "I mean, obviously both can kill you, but that's where the similarities end. The lobbyists were very smart, though. They played to everyone's fears of anything that was prefixed with the word 'nuclear.' So here was the nuclear power lobby—the very cause of America's nuclear anxieties—explaining in graphic detail the dangers of the byproduct of

their very own industry, all in an effort to clear the deck for
a whole new kind of threat. It was perverse. But we fell for it.
By the time they offered their proposal to store nuclear waste,
we were like 'Thank god! A solution!' But obviously it was a
con. They were just shuffling the problem out of sight."

To temporarily shift our attention away from that problem,
the American Nuclear Energy Council began a campaign to
convince Americans that nuclear energy was "110% safe"—
just as long as its waste went elsewhere.

According to Sara Ginsburg's analysis in *Nuclear Waste Disposal*, the American Nuclear Energy Council spent eighteen
months lobbying for the disposal of nuclear waste by deploying "scientific truth squads" throughout the House and Senate, offering to "assist" lawmakers as they "sorted through the
conflicting facts about nuclear energy and waste."

After those tutorials, Representative James Wright, the
Speaker of the House, convinced his fellow lawmakers that
one of the three sites that had been proposed for the waste—a
site that happened to be in his home state of Texas—would
not be suitable for nuclear waste storage. Then Representative Tom Foley, the House majority leader, also convinced his
colleagues that another of those sites—the one that happened
to be in his home state of Washington—couldn't possibly be
suitable for nuclear waste storage.

So the state of Nevada, the home of the third and only
remaining proposed storage site, and the state with the forty-fourth lowest population in the country, did not stand a
chance.

As the spokesperson for the State Department explained

at the time, "There are one million people currently living in Nevada, and 245 million people in the other forty-nine states. . . . Ergo, there are 245 million arguments for sticking it to Nevada, and only one million for putting it somewhere else."

On November 22, 1982, Senator James McClure, the ranking member of the Senate Energy and Natural Resources Committee, introduced a bill that was written by the American Nuclear Energy Council calling for the disposal of nuclear waste on federal land in Nevada. He pushed his bill through committee in an hour and a half, then sent it to the floor for an expedited vote.

It arrived there on the evening of December 21, just hours before the Senate recessed for Christmas break.

Within thirteen minutes, and without a single minute of debate, the Nuclear Waste Policy Act was voted into law.

"I would like to meet the Senator," said one observer that night, "who can tell us what he thinks is even in this bill."

What is in that bill is a plan to dig ninety-seven miles of tunnels into Yucca, spend forty years filling them with 77,000 tons of spent nuclear waste, and then seal the mountain shut until the waste has decomposed. Just ninety miles north of downtown Las Vegas, Yucca Mountain would end up holding at capacity, and if approved, the radiological equivalent of 2 million individual nuclear detonations, about 7 trillion doses of lethal radiation, enough to kill every living resident of Las Vegas, Nevada, four and a half million times over.

Which is why the crowd in Viva was not drinking very much.

Why the bartender tried raising the TV's volume even higher.

Why the pool balls slowly rolled to quiet thuds against the rails, and the one waitress in Viva whispered quietly to herself as she passed beneath the TV with two trays in a rush: "That'a boy, Harry."

Because this was good TV.

Harry Reid was standing on the floor of the Senate Chamber and saying things like "crazy," "unconscionable," and "over my dead body."

The vote that day in the U.S. Senate was indeed important for Vegas. It would officially accept or reject a twenty-year-long study on the effectiveness of Yucca as a potential storage facility for America's nuclear waste.

Called the *Environmental Impact Statement for the Yucca Mountain Project*, the report was 65,000 pages long and included thousands of additional references to hundreds of different studies, all hyperlinked conveniently on two compact disks. If printed out and bound for every member of the Senate, the report would have required 52,000 pounds of paper and could have stretched for over a mile and a half, easily filling the entire floor with two and a half feet of paper.

I didn't notice that much paper on C-SPAN that day, and neither did I see many senators on laptops.

Instead, the senators started their debate by discussing whether this document that none of them possessed contained 252 "unresolved scientific issues," or 293.

Whether this mattered, or whether it did not.

Whether the project was considered by scientists "danger-ous" or "safe" or "more than safe."

Whether an alternative to nuclear waste storage, as reported in an article in *Discover* magazine—and held up by one senator while on the Senate floor—was "possible" or "impossible," whether its name is correctly pronounced "*pryo*-processing" or "*pyra*-processing," and whether an aide in the chamber that day would be willing to check that out.

They discussed its cost of $4 billion.

They discussed its cost of $7 billion.

They even discussed its "free price tag to every Ameri-can taxpayer," because according to someone in the chamber that day, there was "an enormous private energy fund that has been accruing huge interest since the late 1970s in order to pay for projects just like this," which, if he were correct, would have rendered the subsequent discussion about Yucca's projected total cost of "$24 billion" and "$27 billion" and "$38 billion" and "$46 billion" and "$59 billion" and "at least 60 billion" and "100 billion" and "too much" and "we have no other choice" moot.

But the discussion continued nonetheless.

They discussed the 1,000 shipments that were estimated to be needed in order to move the waste to Yucca Mountain by barge. And then the 4,000 by barge that would be needed to move the waste.

The 10,000 by rail, and the 22,000 by rail.

The 50,000 by truck, and the 100,000 by truck.

The routes those shipments would have to take past

"schools," "hospitals," and "nursing homes," and the routes those shipments would never be taking past "schools," "hospitals," and "nursing homes." As well as the point that one senator made that "we don't know the routes this waste is going to take, because no official routes have yet been established. So that map that you have there showing all those routes, sir . . . that . . . I don't know where you got that. You should take that off the floor."

There was even a moment on C-SPAN when Senator Frank Murkowski, the new ranking member of the Senate Energy and Natural Resources Committee, stood on the floor of the Senate Chamber and said, "I would remind the Chamber that the Senate today is not, and I repeat not, voting to finalize its authorization for this nuclear waste repository," at the same time that C-SPAN flashed beneath the senator's image a graphic that read *This resolution authorizes Yucca Mountain, Nevada, for a high-level radioactive waste repository.*

But the most useful demonstration of the confusion that day came in the exchange between Senator Barbara Boxer of California and Senator Harry Reid, during which Senator Boxer, in the midst of a description of the dangerousness of nuclear waste while on the Senate floor, interrupted herself in order to engage Senator Reid in conversation—

SENATOR BOXER: "This waste is so hot that it has
  to be cooled for . . .

[turned briefly toward aide]

For how long? . . . No, I think it's five months. . . .

[turned back toward floor]

Um, I say to my friend from Nevada, Senator Reid . . .
Senator Reid? . . . Um, Senator Reid?"

SENATOR REID: "Yes, my friend from California?"

SENATOR BOXER: "Senator Reid, am I correct in
saying that this waste is so hot that it has to be cooled
down for a very long time, and for how long does
it have to be cooled?"

SENATOR REID: "I will respond to my friend from
California by saying that this month *National Geographic* has a wonderful article on nuclear waste.
Among other things, it confirms what we have
known for a very long time: that nuclear reactors
in America are 97 percent inefficient, which means
that when you put a fuel rod in a nuclear reactor
and then you take it out, it still has 97 percent of its
radioactivity. It's only used 3 percent! Nuclear reactors are so inefficient that after they've been used
they have to be put into cold water to cool down,
and then they can't be taken out of that water for
at least five years. So I would say to my friend from
California, it takes five years."

SENATOR BOXER: "Wow! I thank my friend from
Nevada. I knew that this waste was so hot that it had
to be cooled down for a very long time, but I really
wasn't aware that it was for five years!"

—which was, as I remember it, the only direct clarification
made in the Senate Chamber that day, the only indication of
the presence that afternoon of not so much the reassurance of
veracity as the reassurance of the performance of the process
itself, a promise that—even in the midst of legislation so vast
that its effects on the continent would be influencing the
continent far longer than the country that produced it would
not—the protocol of legislation would not be abandoned,
the performative nature of debate would remain, the fact
that spent nuclear fuel rods in twenty-first-century American reactors required five years rather than five months to
cool down would be noted by stenographers, transcribed and
digitized and bound and archived for as long as such a fact
was determined to be useful.

But the 45,000 tons of nuclear waste that await storage in
the United States, and the 65,000 tons of nuclear waste that
await storage in the United States, and the 47,000 tons of
waste that Yucca Mountain is built to hold, and the 70,000
tons of waste that Yucca Mountain is built to hold, and the
10,000 years that the waste will remain dangerous in the
mountain, and the 24,000 years that the waste will remain
dangerous in the mountain, and the 28 million years that
the waste will remain dangerous in the mountain were facts

whose life spans were limited that day to that of the debate itself, because, as Senator Larry Craig of Idaho put it, "We don't really know what the physical capacity of Yucca Mountain is. This amount that we're all talking about might just be statutory, it might not be physical. Twenty years from now, thirty years from now, I won't be here, I doubt the senior Senator from Nevada will be here, but on some other day, in some other place, if our needs meet our standards and they are strong and they are stable, remember, a statutory limit can be changed if the politics that can argue a change are there to do so."

The politics that were there in the Senate Chamber that afternoon settled on a 60 to 39 vote in favor of approving the Yucca Mountain site, a result that had been predicted two weeks earlier by the Center for Responsive Politics in Washington, D.C., which revealed that during that summer of the Senate's vote on Yucca Mountain over $30 million in individual, PAC, and soft money contributions had been distributed by the nuclear power industry to various U.S. senators, including approximately $56,000 to Senator Blanche Lincoln of Arkansas, $98,000 to Senator Jeff Bingaman of New Mexico, and $109,000 to Senator Mary Landrieu of Louisiana, three of the fifteen Democratic senators who crossed party lines in order to vote in favor of the Yucca Mountain site, and three of the fifteen Democratic senators whose gifts from the nuclear power industry were, on average, twice as high as the gifts that were received by those senators who voted against the project.

"American Nuclear Insurers, Enron, General Electric, Pacific Gas and Electric, Westinghouse . . . I could go on and on," said Senator Harry Reid, just minutes before the vote, reading from a list of what he claimed were the special interest groups that had lobbied for the vote on Yucca Mountain. "These are the people who arrived here today in limousines and Gucci shoes to make sure the vote went through."

He looked up at the Senate gallery where the special interest groups were seated.

"Well go ahead!" he yelled. "Submit your bills, because you've done your jobs well. You have perpetrated a travesty on the American people!"

He threw down his list of special interest groups to the podium, unclipped the microphone from the lapel of his suit, and walked away.

We cheered.

For what, it was hard to say.

By then, the afternoon had begun to stretch thin across the valley, and before the sun would disappear I would decide to live in Vegas.

The winds from the south were blowing palls of white dust, the stock market was low, unemployment rates high, the moon only showing half of itself, and Mars and Jupiter aligned, which isn't particularly rare, and so there is no explanation for the confluence that night of the Senate vote on Yucca Mountain and the death of a boy who jumped from the tower of the Stratosphere Hotel and Casino, a 1,149-foot-high tower in the center of the brown desert valley.

This was around the time the city council in Vegas voted to temporarily ban lap dancing in clubs.

When archeologists found beneath the parking lot of a bar the world's oldest bottle of Tabasco brand sauce.

When a tourist won a game of tic-tac-toe against a chicken.

When someone beat an old man to death with a brick.

It was a day of five deaths from two types of cancer, four from heart attacks, three related to stroke.

It was the day another suicide by gunshot occurred.

The day another suicide by hanging happened.

At a record 114 degrees, it also happened to be one of that summer's hottest days, something that caused the World's Tallest Thermometer to break, raised the price of bottled water to five dollars for eight ounces, and caused a traffic jam on the north end of the Las Vegas Strip as a tourist family traveled toward downtown Las Vegas, rolled over a broken bottle from a homeless woman's cart, blew out a back tire, hit a parked car, and stalled outside the entrance of the Stratosphere Hotel when the jack in the back of their rented Dodge Stratus sank into the heat-softened asphalt of the street.

Some tourists who were there in the traffic jam that night mentioned that they looked up from the crash ahead of them and saw in the sky something fall from the dark, and then through the palms, and then to the city's pavement. Some said they left their cars to look down at what had fallen. Nine of them gave statements of what they saw to the police.

I asked permission to read those statements that the wit-
nesses had given.

I went to the Office of Public Relations to inquire about
security at the Stratosphere's tall tower.

I went to recess, cafeterias, gym class at five schools, trying
to find someone who might have known that dead boy.

Eventually I'd learn his name, and later what he looked
like, and soon enough I would know what kind of car he
had been driving, what church he had attended, what girl
he liked and what girl liked him, his favorite outfit, favorite
movie, favorite restaurant, favorite band, what level belt he
held in Tae Kwon Do, what design he had sketched onto
the wall of his bedroom—very lightly, in pencil—and later
planned to fill in, which drawings of his from art school he
is thought to have been particularly proud of, the nickname
of his car, the two different nicknames his parents had each
given him, his answers to the questions on the last pop quiz
he took in school—

> What is good? What is bad? What does "art" mean to
> you? Now look at the chair on the table in front of you
> and describe it in literal terms

—and of which bottle of cologne among the five this boy kept
in the medicine cabinet down the hall his small bedroom still
smelled, even after his parents had ripped up its carpeting,
thrown out its bed, and emptied its closet of everything but
his art, by the time I first visited them, three months after
his death.

By then, we had learned in Las Vegas that according to the Center for Responsive Politics in Washington, Senator Harry Reid had accepted over $19,000 in campaign contributions from the American Nuclear Energy Council, the lobbying group that Harry Reid had vowed to fight against.

He'd taken $4,000 from Science Applications, an engineering firm with a contract at Yucca.

And he'd received $50,000 from Morrison-Knudsen, a management firm that was bidding at the time on a $3 billion contract at Yucca.

We would also learn in the *Los Angeles Times* that the senator's four sons and his one son-in-law had received $2.5 million in commissions from clients whose interests were served by legislation that Harry Reid had introduced in the U.S. Senate.

And eventually we would hear about a protest that summer that was organized against Reid by the Western Shoshone Indians, a tribe of native people living outside Las Vegas, claiming that they'd been removed by the government years earlier from 24 million acres that began near the city, stretched north across the state, along the western edge of Utah, surrounding all of Yucca.

"What this nation needs," announced President Harry Truman, before removing the Shoshone from their 24 million acres, "is a facility for weapons testing that will ensure the future peace of our nation and its people."

Explaining that this weapons testing facility needed to be built on Western Shoshone Land, Harry Truman then turned to a seventy-year-old peace treaty in order to justify it.

"The said tribes agree," reads the Ruby Valley Treaty of 1863, "that whenever the President of the United States shall deem it expedient for them to abandon the roaming life . . . he is hereby authorized to make reservations for their use.

"It is further agreed," reads the Ruby Valley Treaty, "that the several routes of travel by white men through this country shall be forever free and unobstructed by said tribes . . . and that military posts may be established by the President . . . and station houses may be erected for the convenience of pioneers.

"The parties hereto are also in agreement," continues the same treaty, "that the Shoshone country may be explored and prospected for gold, and that if mines become discovered they may also be explored, and that agricultural settlements may eventually be established . . . and ranches formed . . . and mills erected . . . and timber taken for use."

And, finally, "the tribes hereby acknowledge that they have received from the U.S. government certain provisions and clothing amounting to $2,000," the Ruby Valley Treaty of 1863 concludes, which would suggest to the modern reader, but perhaps not to a mid-nineteenth-century Western Shoshone leader, who may have still been mourning the loss of men in an attack by the U.S. Cavalry just several weeks before, that the 24 million acres at issue in Nevada were in fact already sold, did in fact already belong to the United States government, had in fact already been deemed in the intervening 139 years "worthy of the expedient removal of the Shoshone."

"I'm not a lawyer," said one Shoshone tribe member at the protest that summer, "but I know for sure that if my ancestors had known that a 'military post' meant a bombing range, or that an 'agricultural settlement' meant a waste dump, and that 'free and unobstructed' was really just a code for the total annihilation of my people, then they definitely wouldn't have signed that fucking stupid treaty."

In an admission that the eight tenths of a cent paid by the federal government for each of the Western Shoshone's 24 million acres was not, in hindsight, a fair market price, the United States Indian Land Claims Commission in 1979 awarded the Western Shoshone Indians $26 million for the land they sold to the government, roughly $1, in other words, for every acre of land.

Two thousand dollars for every member of the tribe.

The Shoshone refused this money, however, appealing instead to the Ninth Circuit Court, which eventually ruled in 1994 that payment for an object does not necessarily constitute the sale of that object, and so when the Secretary of the Interior accepted the $26 million on the Western Shoshone's behalf, he did so against their wishes.

By that time, however, the $26 million that was left by the Shoshone in an interest-bearing account with the Department of the Interior was worth in excess of $147 million.

Or $20,000 for every member of the tribe.

"One hundred forty-seven million dollars is a lot different from $26 million," said the chairman of the Western Shoshone Land Claims Committee, a group that was formed to convince the tribe that they ought to take the money. "That money could make a big difference in the lives of our people."

"That money would be gone in a year," said the chairman of the Shoshone National Council, which opposed accepting the money.

The groups therefore agreed to hold a tribal vote that summer, thus settling the stalemate that had been dividing them for years, and exercising, as one member said, "the last right we still possess as an autonomous Indian nation."

But observing them from afar in the meantime that summer, before the vote on Yucca Mountain was scheduled to occur, was Senator Harry Reid, who was quoted as saying in the *Las Vegas Review-Journal* that "the final distribution of this fund has been languishing for twenty-five years, and the Western Shoshone people should not have to wait any longer for it."

That summer, therefore, Harry Reid introduced the Western Shoshone Land Claims Distribution Bill, legislation that eventually passed easily through Congress, won praise from the White House, and automatically delivered checks worth $20,000 to every member of the tribe, thus immediately ending their legal claim to Yucca Mountain, a region that also happened to be important to Barrick Mines, a multi-billion-dollar mining corporation that was a major campaign contributor to Senator Harry Reid, and also the primary shareholder in a new mine near Yucca Mountain—smack in the middle of the Shoshones' disputed land—a find that rendered that region, by the time of Yucca's vote, the single most important source for domestically mined gold.

WHERE

I went to the Yucca Mountain Information Center at the Village Meadows Mall in order to learn more about the proposed waste facility.

When I arrived, a long-skirted teacher from Meadows Junior High School was extending a pointer finger and furrowing her brow.

"We are representing the city of Las Vegas," the teacher told her forty-five students who were lined up against a wall. "So I don't want to see a single shenanigan from you."

The four dozen students against the wall mumbled *Yeah*.

Half of them, the teacher said, were from Accelerated Science. The other half were from a class of Special Education.

We were all there to catch a bus to the Yucca Mountain site, one of the many tours the project offered Vegas locals.

"It's really one of the great perks about living here," said the teacher.

The Information Center was opened in 1998 in an effort to help Las Vegas become acquainted with Yucca Mountain. It's in the middle of a mall, between The Disney Store and Cinnabons, and it has so far served an estimated 94,000 people in the city of Las Vegas.

RADIATION EXISTS, a diorama inside explains . . . *IN NATURE!*

The center is entirely funded by the Department of Energy, the same department that is heading up the Yucca Mountain project.

From a corner of the room, an Educational Outreach Specialist named Blair entered the middle of the Information Center, cleared her throat loudly, exclaimed "Okay!" and then gathered us in front of another diorama.

FACTS, read the banner above the education specialist.

"Today," said Blair, "we're going to talk about misinformation in the Las Vegas media."

She invited us to sit down on some large carpeted cubes, and then began to read from a hypothetical article about a hypothetical spill of nuclear waste on a highway.

"'No waste was spilled during the accident this morning,'" Blair read from the article as she walked among the cubes, "'but one bystander was killed when he climbed over an embankment to view what had occurred, subsequently being struck by a car accidentally.'"

I turned around on my cube to follow Blair as she walked. Behind her was a display called *Nuclear Energy is Green!*

"So," said Blair, "we're gonna try a fun experiment. I'd like you to break up into groups, and each group will be responsible for writing two different headlines for this hypothetical article. The first one should be a headline that describes the facts of the article—making it clear that no one was hurt because of the waste that was spilled—and then the other one should be a headline that sensationalizes the facts. Do you know what 'sensationalize' means? Who watches the local news?"

School programs such as this are part of the center's "Science, Society, and Nuclear Waste" curriculum, a set of lessons it developed in order to "help local teachers provide accurate information about Yucca Mountain." It includes a take-home teacher's manual with 600 pages of text, sixty-one transparencies, seven DVDs, and even a two-hour online workshop that teachers can take for credit. So far, over 900 manuals have been distributed in Vegas, costing the Department of Energy over $800,000.

"It's like an entire course in a box," said the teacher from Meadows Jr. "When you're on a tight budget, as so many teachers are, something like this can be an absolute life-saver for us."

In fact, the Las Vegas superintendent has recently visited the Information Center in order to investigate the possibility of "increasing the Center's level of contribution to our district's curriculum offerings."

Yucca Mountain's influence in Las Vegas public schools became so pronounced by 2006 that U.S. Representative Shelley Berkley introduced an amendment in the House of

Representatives that would ban the Department of Energy from using cartoon characters in any of its curricula.

"The character they call 'Yucca Mountain Johnny' looks too friendly," Berkley complained. "He makes you think that Yucca Mountain is a 'cool' and 'hip' thing, like Joe Camel did with cigarettes."

But as the Department of Energy explained in its defense of the mascot, Yucca Mountain Johnny merely tries to "make more accessible for 5th graders the complex and subtle workings of hydrology, nuclear physics . . . [and] siliciclastic geodynamics."

Or, as another diorama in the center explains, *YUCCA MOUNTAIN IS MADE OF ROCK!*

I pressed the PRESS HERE button to learn more about the rock.

"This makes our own Yucca Mountain range in southwest Nevada an ideal location for nuclear waste storage."

"Isolation," said the recording.

"Stability," it said.

"The guarantee that once it's filled, Yucca Mountain will keep the waste safe, and cool, and dry."

"I was pretty surprised therefore," said Dr. Victor Gilinsky, a physicist from the California Institute of Technology, testifying before Congress about the Yucca Mountain project, "to find myself standing in the middle of this mountain with water dripping out of it and hitting me in the head."

Water, explained Gilinsky, is one of nature's most corrosive substances. It can crack, crush, carry boulders across the planet.

"The existence of water anywhere in this mountain," he said, "will cause corrosion and fissures in the nuclear waste containers, and if that happens the containers could easily start leaking, distributing their contents into the local ecosystem."

In fact, in one of the Department of Energy's own studies on the porousness of Yucca, 63,000 gallons of water were poured over the mountain to see how many years it would take for moisture to reach the level of the proposed repository. The study was ended prematurely, however, when all 63,000 gallons reached the center of the mountain in fewer than three months.

"It's so porous," said Gilinsky, "that this mountain is actually made up of 9 percent water."

Once this was made public, the Department of Energy defended Yucca's failures in such tests by arguing that when the mountain was chosen by Congress in the early 1980s, lawmakers automatically and retroactively lowered any standards for Yucca's suitability, as if inherently acknowledging the site was not ideal.

In other words, noted John Bartlett, the former research director for the Yucca Mountain project, "it was apparent that the original standards for the repository . . . couldn't legitimately be met through the science that we were doing. So the Department of Energy basically changed the rules of its science in order to make it easier for the mountain to comply."

In the fall of 2000, for example, after Yucca Mountain's porousness became impossible to ignore, the Department of

Energy announced that instead of relying on Yucca's geology to protect the nuclear waste, the department was developing a new metal shield that would protect the waste inside the mountain from any kind of moisture. This was hailed by the department itself as an "ingenious solution," a "new evolution in nuclear waste technology," and a "guaranteed success for centuries to come," because the shield would be constructed out of what the department called "a new kind of miracle metal."

Composed of 6 percent nickel, 22 percent chromium, 13 percent molybdenum, and 3 percent tungsten, "Alloy-22" was hailed by the Lawrence Livermore Laboratories—the laboratory that invented it—as "an entirely corrosive-resistant material."

A metallurgist commissioned by the Department of Energy testified that "because these waste canisters will now be protected by a shield of Alloy-22, they will enjoy an impenetrable defense against any of Yucca's dangers."

And the Electric Power Research Institute—the company that was hired by the Department of Energy to test the metal's strength—reported that Alloy-22 "may even have significant resistance to some kinds of magma."

However, when reporters requested copies of the documents that proved these claims, the Department of Energy called their studies "nationally sensitive," and convinced a federal judge to classify them "top secret."

"We strongly urge you to reexamine the current design for this repository," wrote the Nuclear Waste Technical Review

Board, a committee that was formed by Congress to monitor
Yucca's progress.

Based on its own studies, the board believed that the proposed use of Alloy-22 might actually cause moisture inside
Yucca Mountain to react with the salinity that's already in
the air, thus forming a kind of acid that might corrode the
metal shield.

But in a letter from the Department of Energy in response
to this theory, the board's concerns were called "flawed,"
"extreme," and "without scientific support."

So, on the morning of May 12, 2004, while standing
before live cameras at the National Press Club, a geoscientist
from Catholic University in Washington, D.C., and another
geoscientist from the Geosciences Management Company
in Boulder City, Nevada, placed three samples of Alloy-22
in separate glass beakers. They poured over these samples a
mixture of water that contained the same minerals found
inside Yucca Mountain.

Then they stood back and waited.

The home audience watched.

The two geoscientists were silent in their smocks. The
hundred or so members of the Press Club took notes. There
were photographs. Cameras rolling. One of the geoscientists
eventually said, "Okay," and then lifted the first sample of
the metal from its beaker.

The cameras zoomed in, and some flashes went off.

The metal had corroded in twenty-one minutes.

"Don't you agree that your studies at the Yucca Mountain

site have just barely begun to scratch the surface of this enormous technical problem?" a member of the Review Board
asked a scientist from Yucca at a hearing about the mountain
on Capitol Hill.

"I don't know," said the scientist, "if I would say 'barely.'"

In its earlier incarnation as the Atomic Energy Commission, the Department of Energy oversaw the development of
the first atomic bomb at the Los Alamos National Laboratory,
a facility that was discovered to have dumped over 10,000
gallons of nuclear waste every single day between 1946 and
1957 in an area of desert that's now called "Acid Canyon," a
region of New Mexico that contains 600 times more radioactive contaminants than any other place on Earth.

In 1970, another project overseen by the Department of
Energy was revealed to have intentionally released the equivalent of over 340,000 lethal doses of radiation over northeast
Washington in a study that it called "The Green Run Experiment," the purpose of which was to track radioactivity in the
event of a nuclear strike. Because the project was top secret,
however, local residents were never informed of its potential
hazards.

"Anything that we saw that was odd, or that we'd call in
and ask about," said one resident in an interview in 1990,
"they explained was swamp gas and wouldn't be a problem.
When they drove up our driveway and asked for specimens
of dead animals, or if they took dirt samples from our gar-
dens, they'd say, 'We're monitoring this to make sure that
you're safe.' And so we'd ask, 'From what? Are you finding

anything?' And they'd say, 'No, but if we do we'll let you know.'"

But the Department of Energy never did let them know, and twenty-seven people died eventually there of cancer.

And most recently, documents released through the Freedom of Information Act revealed that from 1948 to 1971 the Department of Energy dumped over 200 billion gallons of waste into the soil around Washington's Hanford Nuclear Reservation. An investigation by the state's Government Affairs Committee estimated that the amount of waste that had been dumped at Hanford could fill a lake that was roughly the size of Manhattan, three and a half stories deep.

"Let me be perfectly frank," wrote one retired general of the United States Air Force in a letter he addressed to the Department of Energy, "this is unforgivably scandalous."

By then, a report from the United States Geological Survey had declared that the Department of Energy's experiments were "generally . . . inept."

A report from the Nuclear Energy Commission found their science "exceedingly faulty."

And the General Accounting Office, the office of independent congressional oversight, called the Department of Energy's funding—which was twice as large as Social Security's, thirteen times larger than the Department of Education's, and thirty-nine times larger than the Department of Justice's—"vulnerable to waste, fraud, mismanagement, and abuse."

"Maybe if we can find out where all this money is going,"

said the governor of Nevada in 1993, "we can put the waste in there, and then we won't have any problems."

But the problems with the Department of Energy continued in Nevada. In 1998, the California Institute of Technology revealed that Yucca Mountain was stretching, seismically, ten times faster than anyone had thought. Based on satellite surveillance studies, the institute estimated that the entire mountain was likely to move almost fifty full feet over the next 1,000 years. In addition, since 1994, the department had known that running directly through Yucca Mountain was a 900-foot-wide earthquake zone that was called the Sundance fault. It had known that crisscrossing just beneath it was a fault called Ghost Dance. And it had known that Yucca Mountain's own chief geologist, Jerry Szymanski, had discovered as early as 1988 that any kind of fault movement in or around the mountain could cause what he was calling "massive upwelling," a surge of steaming water from deep within the Earth that could flood the site's repository and corrode the waste's containers, sending their nuclear waste into the desert's ecosystem, the nearby water table, and eventually into the city of Las Vegas itself.

"The point is that the Yucca Mountain scientists all have kids, just like you," Blair said to the class in the Information Center, "so that's why they're busy trying to prove that Yucca Mountain will be safe."

She passed out her final exercise to the children that morning: a plastic bag of Silly Putty, Kitty Litter, Styrofoam peanuts, and a small water bottle that was labeled "waste container."

"Now," she said, "let's pretend that these water bottles are the same metal containers that the waste is going to be stored in. I want you to build a waterproof seal around your waste to prove that these containers won't leak into the mountain. Then I'm going to pour water over each of your containers in order to determine who made the tightest seal."

One student picked up a plastic bag and asked, "Wait, which one's the waste? The peanuts?"

"No, honey," said Blair, walking over and leaning, "the Kitty Litter's the waste, the Styrofoam peanuts are your protective barrier."

"Then what's the Silly Putty for?" another student asked.

"The scientists call that 'Alloy-22.' It's a very strong metal," Blair said, sitting down.

"So we're being graded on whether or not the Kitty Litter will last?" a student asked while smashing Silly Putty to his face.

"No, stupid," said a girl sitting across the table, "it's based on how much the litter is going to leak out. Duh."

"Well, we don't want it to leak," Blair said, standing up.

"Well, yeah," said the girl. "I know."

"So it's based on how long the Silly Putty can last?" the boy with the putty on his face asked again.

"It's based on what you think will last the longest," said Blair.

"So is the bottle biodegradable?" a different boy asked.

"It's not a bottle," said Blair. "It's your container, remember?"

"Then how long can the container last?" asked the Silly Putty boy.

"Well, that's the point," said Blair. "You've got to figure that out."

"How long does it have to last for?" the Putty boy asked.

"Ten thousand years," Blair said, sitting down.

About 10,000 years ago, the Pleistocene was ending. Sheets of ice were stretched over Greenland and Canada and Oregon and Michigan and Ohio and New York and Maine. They covered Finland and Russia, Germany and Britain. The Andes were fully covered, and the Caucasus were fully covered, and even the Himalayas, to their peaks, were covered up.

Between these sheets were 5 million scattered human beings, living in small groups in which they mainly hunted, gathered, and had just begun to farm.

They had dogs but not sheep.

Goats, but not cows.

Among them were wooly mammoths, as well as saber-tooths.

There were bears that could stand almost twelve feet tall.

There were brand-new species of firs in the ground.

There was prairie grass in deserts.

A sea inside Iraq.

And there is even some evidence, according to cave paintings, that human beings were living side by side with were-wolves.

Back then we spent time making knives out of stones. Spears and harpoons and arrows and bows. We wore necklaces and bracelets and sometimes paint tattoos, and in India and Syria and Iran and Pakistan we ate lentils, peas, fava beans, wheat. In China, we ate apples. We had corn in northern Chile. Grapes in southern Turkey. Plums on the Nile's shore.

What we hadn't yet discovered on the planet, however, were oranges and cotton and mangoes and olives and squash and tomatoes and dates.

We had not yet found peaches.

Nor yet the potato.

We had not yet found sugar, chocolate, almonds, or wine. Not watermelons, bananas, strawberries, or limes.

There wouldn't be any paper for 6,000 years. No coffee beans or tea for 7,000 years. No soap for 8,000. No glass or books or currency for more.

It was before there was a Bible, a Koran, a Chinese *Book of Changes*. It was around the time the last dragons in Sweden disappeared. Around the time Atlantis was destroyed by a flood. And it's when 45 percent of Americans believe, according to a Gallop poll from 2003, that God first created the Earth.

On the bus that morning to Yucca, someone asked Blair why 10,000 was picked.

"Well," she said, "they picked ten thousand years because that's how long the half-life of the waste is going to be. Who knows what a half-life is?"

She extended her arms with her palms up before her and waited with her eyes for an answer.

The girl who asked the question put her headphones back on.

"Well, think of a half-life as nature's egg timer," Blair said, standing in the aisle of the bus with a mic. "After the buzzer goes off, the half-life is over, and all of the radioactive elements are safe."

Someone's PlayStation slid down the aisle of the bus.

A boy stood up, walked down the aisle, said *Hey* to some girls on his way to the game, picked it up, turned around, then walked back up the bus.

"Yucca Lady," someone said, with his hood up over his head, "is this bus gonna show any movies?"

The half-life of iodine-131, a common compound in commercial spent nuclear waste, is approximately eight and a half days, which does in fact mean that the material in that time will lose half of its power, but it does not mean that it loses its lethality. Even after fifty years of cooling, for example, the surface dose rate of the typical nuclear waste cocktail would be 8,000 rem per hour, which is 100,000 curies.

Which is, more simply put, still dangerous enough to kill someone within five minutes of exposure.

Most environmental scientists don't consider radioactive materials "safe," therefore, until they've been dormant for ten times their projected half-life.

One day I asked the librarian at the Information Center why a period of 10,000 years had been set for Yucca Mountain.

"Good question," she said, nodding her head and squinting. "So, let's see. . . . Hmm. . . . Well, okay . . . Umm . . . I think that's gonna be a question for someone at DOE."

I went to the regional office of the Department of Energy in order to ask my question about the 10,000-year-long period. But the spokesman they sent down to speak with me in the lobby said that the period had been set for them by the Environmental Protection Agency.

I drove south to the local office of the EPA, but the woman on the intercom at the locked front door told me that my request would have to be in writing.

I wrote to the EPA in Las Vegas three times, and finally was told in an e-mail that the 10,000-year-long period for the Yucca Mountain project was established by the Yucca Mountain Development Act of 2002.

I looked up that act, which is one page long, and only found a reference in it to another act of Congress, the Energy Policy Act of 1992.

According to the Energy Policy Act of 1992, "scientists of the National Academies are to consider whether it is possible to make scientifically supportable predictions of the probability that the repository's engineered or geologic barriers will be breached as a result of human intrusion over a period of 10,000 years."

So I asked the National Academies of Science how it determined that 10,000-year-long period. The Academies is a nonprofit consortium of scientific advisers that was established by Abraham Lincoln in the early 1860s for the purpose of "counseling the government on matters of technology and dedicated to the furtherance of knowledge for the American citizenry." But when I reached the librarian at the National Academies, he sent me to the office of the National Research Council.

At the National Research Council, which was chartered in 1913 in order to help Congress monitor the activities of

the National Academies of Science, I asked a woman in Public Affairs about the 10,000-year-long period, and she told
me that the best people to talk to about that would be the
National Research Council's Board on Radioactive Waste
Management.

The Board on Radioactive Waste Management at the
National Research Council is a twenty-member committee
of geologists, nuclear physicists, and chemical engineers that
has been commenting on the plan to store waste at Yucca
Mountain since the late 1980s, so I asked one of their secre-
taries about the 10,000-year-long period, and she sent me to
the Radioactive Waste Management Board's Committee on
the Technical Bases for Yucca Mountain Standards.

Chaired by Robert Fri, a scholar at Resources for the
Future, an environmental policy group in Washington, D.C.,
the Committee on the Technical Bases for Yucca Mountain
Standards has written 145 reports on Yucca Mountain.

"Hi, sir," I said, when I reached chairman Fri. "Thank
you so much for giving me a second of your time. . . . First, I
guess I'm just wondering if you're the right guy to ask about
the ten-thousand-year-long period that's been set for Yucca
Mountain."

"I could try to help, sure," said committee chairman Fri.

"Great," I said. "Then the only other thing I'm trying to
figure out is why the time scale for the waste that's headed
for Yucca Mountain was set at ten thousand years. I mean, is
there a reason why ten thousand specifically was picked?"

"Well, yes," said the chairman. "But, also, no."

"Yes and no?" I said.

"Right," he said. "In other words, there were definitely reasons why we chose the time frame we did."

"Okay."

"But ten thousand years isn't the time frame we chose."

"It's not?"

"No."

"What happened?"

"It's complicated."

"Could you explain it?" I asked.

"Well, basically," said the chairman, "Yucca Mountain is what happened."

In a study of the mountain entitled *Technical Bases for Standards at Yucca Mountain, Nevada*, chairman Fri and his committee originally wrote:

> "The reason for imposing a time frame on the Yucca Mountain project would be to ensure that there are no significant health risks to humans during the waste's storage. Taking into consideration that some potentially harmful exposures may still be possible several hundred thousand years following the mountain's closure, we therefore recommend that a time frame be established that includes those periods of peak potential risks . . . which could be on the order of a million years or more."

But stability at Yucca Mountain couldn't be guaranteed for as long as a million years, so somewhere within that long

chain of federal policy wranglers the time frame for secur-
ing the nuclear waste at Yucca Mountain was decreased by
approximately 99 percent.

"What we're dealing with here," explained Bob Halstead,
a nuclear waste consultant for the state of Nevada, "is an
exercise in planning for a nuclear catastrophe that is fundamentally rhetorical. It's theatrical security, because the prepa-
rations that are being made by the Department of Energy
have no real chance of succeeding. They satisfy the public,
however, because they're a symbol of control. Ten thousand
years sounds like a long time, right? But in terms of actually
doing what that mountain needs to do, ten thousand years is
useless. This waste is going to be deadly for tens of millions
of years."

Bob Halstead was hired by the state of Nevada in the late
1990s after he successfully defended other states from propos-
als for waste repositories.

"In reality," he said, "I've come to believe that the greatest
threat we face at Yucca Mountain isn't actually posed by the
waste's half-life. The biggest threat we face is the transportation of this shit."

Seventy-seven thousand tons of spent nuclear waste currently await disposal at nuclear power plants. It's estimated
that it would take 108,000 individual shipments just to truck
it all out to Yucca, 1,000 pounds at a time, carried in shipping
casks that have never been subjected to full-scale safety tests.

"Why haven't they ever been tested?" Bob asked me over

the phone. "Because the Nuclear Regulatory Commission doesn't require full-scale tests of nuclear waste containers. And why don't they require full-scale safety tests of these things? Nobody really knows. But I suspect it's because none of these nuclear waste containers could actually pass a safety test."

In "Testing to Failure: Design for Full-Scale Fire and Impact Tests for Spent Fuel Shipping Casks," a report that Bob delivered at the 32nd Annual Waste Management Symposium, a single shoulder-launched missile was shown to be able to breach the wall of a waste shipping cask, deeply penetrating its innermost core, and ejecting just 1 percent of the cask's cargo into the atmosphere, which is enough to produce 21,000 curies of radiation.

"One percent might not sound like a lot," said Bob, "but one percent is about all you need to do massive damage in Vegas."

For example, imagine a power plant somewhere in the United States where pencil-thin fuel rods are being removed from their reactor, chopped into nuggets, packed into casks, and then driven aboard a truck across the U.S. Highway system, day after day, for the next four decades.

During that time, the trucks carrying the nuclear waste will pass through thirty-one states, 700 different counties, and within three and a half miles of 120 million Americans.

During those forty years, they'll travel through Chicago every seventeen hours.

Through St. Louis every fifteen.

Every thirteen through Denver, every ten through Omaha, every seven through Los Angeles, and every five through Salt Lake City.

They'll arrive in Las Vegas in 3,000 yearly truckloads. Two hundred fifty monthly ones, fifty-five weekly ones, eight or nine daily ones. One load every two hours and forty-eight minutes converging with the traffic of Las Vegas, Nevada, at the intersection of Interstates 15 and 80 in an area that is known for exchanges so confusing that commuters simply call it the Las Vegas "spaghetti bowl."

From there, the waste will begin the last 100 miles of its journey, a journey that's been called by the Radioactive Waste Management Associates, a private research firm that conducted a study of the potential routes that this waste would take to Yucca, "the most dangerous hundred miles of the waste's entire journey."

Its report, *Worst Case Credible Nuclear Transportation Accidents*, is a study that hypothesizes the outcome of an accident with one of the waste transportation trucks headed for Yucca Mountain. The report imagines a day during those four decades of shipments. By then, the number of registered cars in the city of Las Vegas is estimated to be about 2.5 million, approximately one eighth of which will travel through the spaghetti bowl each day, 30,000 during commuter time, 10,000 each hour, or 85 cars every 31 seconds in the ramps and lanes and soft narrow shoulders of the Las Vegas spaghetti bowl highway.

Eighty-five cars with eighty-five drivers and eighty-five chances of making mistakes. Eighty-five cars that could possibly skid, and eighty-five cars that could possibly roll, and eighty-five cars that might also pile, bunched behind a truck on its way to Yucca Mountain that has somehow flipped, and somehow crashed, and somehow caught on fire.

According to the *Worst Case Credible* report, diesel trucks become engulfed in flames when their tanks reach a core temperature of 1,832 degrees Fahrenheit, while nuclear waste casks usually become engulfed at 1,732 degrees Fahrenheit, rupturing approximately thirty minutes afterward, and "particularizing their pellets into respirable aerosol," according to *Reexamination of Spent Fuel Shipping Risk Estimates*, a study by the Nuclear Regulatory Commission. This means that in such a hypothetical scenario on the spaghetti bowl highway, the city of Las Vegas would have thirty minutes to evacuate the occupants of those eighty-five cars that are jammed around the truck that's flipped over on the highway.

However, as is pointed out in the *Worst Case Credible* report, the Las Vegas spaghetti bowl is an elevated highway and is therefore only accessible by way of its on-ramps. The time it would take for rescue units to reach this accident is estimated to be far longer than for any other location in Vegas.

Meanwhile, five minutes will have passed on the spaghetti bowl highway, where 630 cars are now jammed around the truck.

There are also two copters, some rubbernecking drivers, participants in the accident who are honking and milling, two

SUV drivers who are starting to fight, a dead driver in the truck, and five more minutes of confusion on the highway—fifteen minutes in all since the accident occurred—where 2,200 more cars are now jammed, blocking access to the accident for the firefighters arriving.

It's a scene that stretches roughly 500 feet wide, 300 feet farther than their fire hoses reach.

The firefighters on the scene will decide to leave their truck, moving on foot with extinguishers on their backs, and ordering the occupants of the many trafficked cars to evacuate their vehicles and run away from the fire, to which all of the occupants in the spaghetti bowl's cars—an estimated 7,000 people by now—will respond by immediately exiting their cars at the same time that the container ruptures.

No one on the spaghetti bowl realizes this, though, since the irradiated plume that escapes from the cask is colorless and odorless and leaves the scene on the currents of the traffic copters' gusts. It drifts with the wind at a rate of ten feet per second, heading east toward the Strip, and the Strip's largest hotels, less than 2,000 feet from the spaghetti bowl highway. One of these structures, a thirty-two-story hotel of 7,000 guests and 4,000 rooms and 150 million cubic feet of air, begins sucking bits of the irradiated plume through its vents, distributing to its rooms and casinos and kitchens a mixture of diesel and strontium and cesium and iodine and carbon monoxide.

However, according to the "Las Vegas Hazardous Materials Response Plan," the hotel's daytime operations manager will not yet have been contacted by local Vegas officials because the first instruction in the Hazardous Response Plan is that a team of technicians assemble at the scene, determine whether or not radiation has been leaked, establish a perimeter, evacuate civilians, and then, an estimated twenty-five minutes later—or fifty-five minutes after the accident occurred—order local businesses, hospitals, and schools to shut down their external vents.

When the hotel's daytime manager finally gets word of this, he'll turn off the hotel's exterior intakes, turn on the building's recycling air fans, and seal into the hotel a mixture of diesel and strontium and cesium and carbon monoxide. At this point, the air that will be hovering outside the hotel will be cleaner than what is inside.

Three people in the hotel will die immediately of exposure. Within a year, another ninety-four may die from radiation poisoning. Over the following fifty years, an estimated 1,000 guests from the hotel that day could develop some form of cancer.

Ten days after the accident, the city of Las Vegas will remain closed at its borders. A team of black copters with gamma-ray detectors will fly overhead to evaluate the damage. The level of radiation registering in the city will be 50,000 millirem, 49,000 higher than the EPA allows.

According to a study by the Sandia National Laboratories entitled *Site Restoration: Estimation of Attributable Costs from Plutonium-Dispersal Accidents*, a spill such as the one on the spaghetti bowl highway would have "a decontamination factor higher than 10," which means that it would be more destructive than any other spill that the lab has yet considered, affecting an area of 17 square miles, 700,000 people, and causing $189 billion in damage.

The study's evaluation of such a hypothetical spill is that "clean-up would not be possible with today's present technology."

It continues:

> "The only two possibilities for dealing with such a heavily contaminated area are to raze and rebuild the site, or to evacuate it entirely, declaring the area uninhabitable. Under the first scenario, sidewalks, streets, and buildings would have to be removed . . . while the second scenario involves the permanent quarantine of the heavily contaminated areas, resulting in the relocation of hotels, casinos, places of employment, and residents."

"We'd forfeit Las Vegas to the desert," explained Bob. "The city would no longer exist."

But the Department of Energy's own evaluation of the effects of such a spill are far less pessimistic. In fact, the Department of Energy does not believe that such a spill would even occur. In its own studies for Yucca Mountain, the Department of Energy considered "reasonably foreseeable incidents" during the shipping of its waste to Yucca, but not the "worst case credible" ones. According to the

DOE's estimates, therefore, this would result in a "1-in-10 million" chance that Yucca's waste will be involved in a serious accident, a probability that's within acceptable risk limits for large-scale federal projects.

Yet, when it comes to a place like the city of Las Vegas, where nine deliveries of nuclear waste could be arriving every day, those 1–in–10 million odds over a forty-year period are more accurately represented by a figure of 1–in–27,000 odds, thus making the possibility of a nuclear accident in Vegas higher than the possibility of striking it rich in a casino.

"It's dangerous to concentrate so much on probabilities that we forget about possibilities," Lee Clarke has written. "After all, we all like to believe that chance is in our favor. But chance is also often against us. Things that have never happened before happen all the time."

Lee Clarke is a sociologist at Rutgers University who specializes in planning for improbable possibilities.

"Refusing to keep a proper balance between the probable and the possible can skew our ability to recognize legitimate dangers," he said. "Catastrophes are common, failures are a part of life. Airplanes crash. Houses explode. More people die in U.S. hospitals every year from medical errors than they do from industrial accidents, car accidents, or AIDS. In the PBS documentary *Meltdown at Three Mile Island*, the director of the Nuclear Regulatory Commission said that 'within the NRC no one really thought that you could have a core meltdown. Ours was more of a *Titanic* mentality. We thought that the plant was so well designed that you couldn't possibly have major core damage.' And he was right. The possibility of having all the things that went wrong at Three Mile Island simultaneously happen was very small. But they still happened. And nuclear officials ignored that possibility at our peril. That's the problem with our modern approach to risk assessment. It's based on 'probablistic' thinking—like *what's the likelihood that this nuclear plant will experience a melt down?*—as opposed to worst case credible thinking, which is 'possibilistic'—*what happens if this plant has a really, really bad day?"*

In that case, the steel girder straps on the spaghetti bowl's ramps would have to be removed, scrubbed, tagged, and then stored indeterminately in a repository all their own.

Every black span of asphalt would also have to go.

The green reflective street signs.

The bolts connecting each sign to the spaghetti bowl's sides.

Every nut that secures the bolts.

Every washer that goes between them.

Every traffic lamp and bulb and post.

Every sidewalk square and concrete curb.

Every newspaper stand.

Every call girl ad.

Every chunk of gum, every splotch of gum, every wet and dry and long-gone lugie. Every cigarette butt and crushed-up glass and puddle of vomit and urine and shit. Every blade of grass at the base of the posts of the signs of the Strip's hotels.

And every hotel, for that matter.

All pavilions of lawn and lagoons of light and porte cocheres and driveways. All the heavy wooden stands with the little brassy hooks and the hanging numbered valet tickets.

The railing of iron you grip up the steps of the indoor and outdoor carpet.

The hinges of the door and the glass in the panes and the smudges from the hands that touched them.

And the small chandeliers in the foyer.

And the large chandeliers in the lobby.

And the vases of the flowers not fresh anymore on the ledges of *CHECK-IN HERE*. And the ashtrays etched with the hotel logo, the ballpoint pens with the hotel logo, the notepads stamped with the hotel logo, the sand in the tray on the trashcan covers impressed with the hotel logo.

The white button UP on the elevator door. The CLOSE DOOR button on the inside door. The black lettered sign in the elevator car for *INSPECTION CERTIFICATE ON FILE IN OFFICE.*

The antique table where the elevator stops in the hall with the white marble top.

The gold-gilded mirror behind it.

The chair rails nailed along each floor's hallway, the sconces hanging down each floor's hallway, the room numbers glued beside each room's door, the switchplates inside them, the stacks of white towels, the shower caps, sewing kits, emery boards, cotton balls, shoe mitts and Q-tips and combination bottles of conditioning shampoo.

And all the conditioning shampoo.

All the body lotions, shower gels, imported milled soaps and eaux de toilette and tissues and bathmats and dryers and irons and toilets and sinks and tiles.

All 1,987 pages in the local Las Vegas phone book. All 117 million pages in all of that hotel's phone books. All 928 billion pages inside all the phone books in every nightstand in each of the rooms in all the hotels in the city that must be destroyed.

Which means "Action Demolition," and "Amigos Demolition," and "Budget Demolition," and "Dirt Man Demolition," and "Disaster Kleen-Up Vegas," and "Ned's City Clearing," and "Roland's Excavation," and "World-Wide Deconstruction," and "Reconstruction Center," and "Nature Redefined," and THE ONE MAN CHOSEN BY CELEBRITIES FAMOUS ATHLETES AND EQUALLY SELECTIVE PEOPLE LIKE YOU DR. JULIO GARCIA THE ONLY COSMETIC SURGEON IN THE CITY OF LAS VEGAS WITH A COLLEGE DEGREE IN ART, and "Body By Biff," "New Body For You," the "International Institute of Permanent Cosmetics," the "Vegas Skin Institute," "Plastic Surgery Institute," "Repair Surgery Institute," THE ONLY PRIVATE INSTITUTE IN THE CITY OF LAS VEGAS THAT SPECIALIZES IN EVERY COSMETIC PROCEDURE and HAVE A FABULOUS FACE and HAVE A SHAPELY BODY and HAVE BEAUTIFUL BREASTS with SAME-DAY EVENING AND WEEKEND APPOINTMENTS and STOP DON'T LOOK

FURTHER I'M CUTE AND PETITE and I'M NOT AN ESCORT AGENCY and "Brandy" NOT AN AGENCY and "Aimee" NOT AN AGENCY and "Trevor" NOT AN AGENCY and "Debbi and Dan" DOUBLE DOWN WITH US and IS IT BOB OR IS IT BOBBI and BUY ONE GET ONE EXOTIC DANCERS and LOWEST PRICE DANCERS and WE'LL COME TO YOU and FREE BRUNETTE DANCER WITH EACH ORDERED BLONDE and FULL SERVICE TEENS and TOP DOWN GIRLS and BACK STREET BOYS and THIRD WORLD GIRLS and MATURE MARRIED MOMS and IMPRIS-ONED WITH IVANA and BARELY LEGAL TWINKS and MULATTO COLLEGE CO-ED and JUST OUT OF SCHOOL and JUST HAVING FUN and all drapes and all spreads and all Pringles and pretzels and cashews and gum-mies and V-8's and sunblock and vodka and trail mix and facemasks and card decks and terrycloth robes with the hotel logo, and SEALED FOR YOUR POTECTION "safe inti-macy kits," and a copy of *Showbiz* on every nightstand, and PLACED BY THE GIDEONS inside the nightstand.

And after all the rooms, the suites.

And after all of those, the ballrooms.

And after all the ballrooms, the fitness centers, the late-night kitchens, the laundry rooms, switchboards, future res-ervations: the pool views, garage views, the mountains in the distance.

WHY

I drove with my mom and a friend of hers for an hour north of Vegas, past a dusty new development just emerging from the sand, past a NASCAR racing stadium's 100,000 empty seats, past a turnoff for what its guidepost called "The Loneliest Highway in America."

"Do you see it yet?" asked my mother's friend, a man named Joshua Abbey.

"What are we looking for?" I asked.

Josh pointed straight into the windshield as he drove.

"The feet should be south, the head toward the north, the arms kinda folded across his chest like a mummy."

"Are we looking for a dead guy?" asked my mom through binoculars.

"Well, sleeping," Josh said. "Or, yeah . . . dead. It's called Mummy Mountain. But I prefer to think he's sleeping."

We drove closer, toward his feet, then spiraled up around them.

One thousand feet up.

Two thousand feet up.

With ski poles and knapsacks, 500 feet by foot.

Past creosote colonies and giant stands of spruce trees and Joshua saying by way of nothing, "Don't ask me what anything's called. My father was into the names of things, but I don't care about names."

"Your father?" asked my mom.

"Yeah," Josh replied.

"Was your dad an activist too?"

"My father was Edward Abbey."

"Your father was Edward Abbey?"

"Yeah. You didn't know that?"

His father, Edward Abbey, moved Joshua and his family to Las Vegas in the sixties, hoping to secure a government job as a welfare case worker. This was before *The Monkey Wrench Gang*, before *Desert Solitaire*. It was before the mythology of Edward Abbey had reason to even exist.

"He was just 'Dad' at that point," Josh said as we climbed. "Or at least he was a good facsimile of one. He was good at being facsimiles."

Abbey often claimed on the jackets of his books that he was "born in Home, Pennsylvania" and that he "lived in Oracle, Arizona." But neither of those claims was true.

"He liked the prophetic suggestion of those biographical details," one biographer wrote. "But of course, it has to be said that there was very often a gap between the rhetoric of Abbey's writing and the realities of his life."

Indeed, the man who was responsible for inspiring a whole generation of environmental activists often left cars to their demise in protected wild preserves, tossed beer cans onto highways, abandoned used tires in pristine National Parks.

And also, Josh said, he was kind of an asshole.

Married five times and unfaithful innumerably, Abbey was confronted by his first wife, Josh's mother, after she learned of an ongoing affair.

"When my mother asked him about it, he just stood up, grabbed a suitcase, and left without a word. I didn't see him for another ten years. No child support. No 'sorry.' Nothing. Just gone."

Josh stepped off the trail and briefly pointed into nothing.

A single bristlecone pine tree sprouted from a rock.

Limb-gnarled and orange, crisp-barked and leafless, the bristlecone is the oldest living organism on Earth. It survives millennia longer than anything else around it because it slowly shuts down whole portions of itself, then efficiently sends nutrients to its most crucial parts. It's not unusual for the only living piece of a bristlecone to be a single green limb thrust out of a hollow trunk.

"You'd never know that most of these bristlecones are thousands of years older than even redwoods," said Josh.

Beyond the tree a haze of heat listed over desert. Fifty wavy miles. Then highway strip. Then miles. Then black-encrusted ridges bumping silently from Earth.

"So," Josh said. "What do you think?"

"Of what?"

"Of Yucca," he said.

"Where?"

"Straight ahead."

"Where?"

"That low range."

"Really?" I asked.

Yucca Mountain isn't pretty. And it also isn't large. From far away, the mountain's just a squat bulge in the middle of the desert, essentially just debris from a bigger, stronger mountain that erupted millions of years ago and hurled its broken pieces into piles across the earth.

The Shoshone say that Yucca is the carcass of a snake, a giant desert creature that was trying to find a drink, collapsed there in exhaustion, rotted as it died.

"Better a cruel truth," Edward Abbey once wrote, "than a comfortable delusion."

So we climbed the mountain higher, and the spruce began to wither, and the bristlecones to gather, and the pitch of trail sharpened, and the edge of ridge straightened, and the soil whisked off limestone sheets and loosened them to shingles.

Joshua pulled my mother quickly in front of him and said, "Watch it here, the path is narrow," as the path ahead began to fade, and then it disappeared.

Originally, the plan in the U.S. was to recycle nuclear waste. We'd reprocess all our fuel rods at individual plants, then reuse them over and over again, indefinitely, for power. But doing that would have also produced a pure form of plutonium, a byproduct of the process that's inevitable and dangerous and ultimately was deemed too risky during fears of nuclear proliferation.

So the next plan was to bury the waste in trenches underwater, weighted down in teardrops that would sink into the Earth. In the late 1970s, however, a Soviet nuclear sub accidentally released three armed warheads while traveling near Alaska in the Bering Sea, nearly contaminating 187 square miles of international ocean. So a worldwide sea treaty outlawed that proposal.

Then, in the 1980s, a new plan was developed to launch the waste on rockets that would crash into the Sun. But when climatologists explained that a single rocket accident could permanently irradiate Earth's entire atmosphere, that plan was also internationally banned.

There was a plan involving "garden mulch," but no one took it seriously.

There was a plan to seal it in permafrost. But the permafrost is melting.

The Chinese proposed burning their waste in tunnels underground, vitrifying it permanently beneath that nation's streets.

"We have a responsibility to the future," wrote Helge Thue, a Scandinavian philosopher who spoke on the issue of disposing nuclear waste at a conference entitled "Ethics in the Age of Nuclear Power." "Environmental regulations such as those being proposed for burying nuclear waste are fundamental to human society because what they do is protect the lives of future generations by prohibiting us from prematurely destroying their chance for an existence. The worldwide burial of this nuclear waste guarantees our descendants a right to their own futures."

"Why are we assuming," asked another ethicist, "that it's better to make an investment in burying this waste than it would be to spend that money to help people now? Why is the life of someone not yet alive more valuable than someone who's dying from poverty?"

An investment of $210 for an immunization could save somebody's life in Indonesia, for example. Fifty dollars could prevent a measles death in Cameroon. And a ten-cent tablet to purify water could save someone from dying in Mozambique.

"A single dollar," he said, "invested in a trust fund at 3 percent interest would yield more than $6 trillion in less than a thousand years. Why not send our descendants a giant trust fund, therefore, providing them with the resources to deal intelligently with this waste? Surely their technology will be more advanced than ours. And that way we can keep the majority of this money to spend on people now."

In 5,000 years, that single dollar would eventually yield $4,004,537,935,765,068 in interest for our long-term descendants, a figure that is increased by another twenty-four zeros—

16 quatturordecillion, 358 tredecillion, 287 duodecillion, 111 undecillion, 891 decillion, 358 nonillion, 534 octillion, 699 septillion, 727 sextillion, 343 quintillion,

43 quadrillion, 255 trillion, 558 billion, 219 million, 536 thousand, and 75 dollars

—if invested for the full 10,000 years.

And if we hypothetically were to invest just a billion dollars of Yucca's total estimated cost—or 1/100th of its overall budget—we would have a gift to give them that is 50 zeros long—

16 sexdillion, 358 quidecillion, 287 quatturodecillion, 111 tredecillion, 890 duodecillion, 364 undecillion, 266 decillion, 369 ninillion, 153 octillion, 4 septillion, 908 sextillion, 853 quintillion, 510 quadrillion, 524 trillion, 45 billion, 885 million, 440 thousand, 800 dollars, and 41 cents

—plus an extra $99 billion to spend on ourselves, thirty-three times more than the United Nations' budget.

"The problem that we're dealing with," notes Peter Van Wyck, a professor of Communication Studies at Concordia University, "is that the threat of buried nuclear waste doesn't feel real to us. That's why there's a debate going on about whether this is even necessary. It's the difference between experiencing a natural disaster and a technical one, which is the difference between having a story that we know how to read, and having one that breaks the rules of any narrative we know."

In a natural disaster, Van Wyck explained, there is a rapid

punctuation of events: a sudden rise of water during a flood, conventionally indicating a "beginning," then a point at which the water crests in the narrative's "middle," and finally a period when the water recedes, which naturally signals an "end."

"But a technical disaster, like Chernobyl's meltdown," said Van Wyck, "is much more difficult to follow because it doesn't adhere to the conventions of plot. It has a definite beginning, and probably a climax, but its end is indeterminate because it's hard for us to know when such disasters have concluded. . . . It causes the arc of these tragedies to feel incomplete. For the residents around Chernobyl, of course, the event that caused their suffering may never significantly end, but for the rest of us something like that is over as soon as we fail to remember it."

To avoid this happening with nuclear waste, the conference attendees suggested disposing the waste that was headed for Yucca Mountain in a way that would cause it to "scream louder than anything we've ever done as a species . . . more profoundly, more symbolically . . . the kind of message understood by a whole culture at once."

Which is when the idea of building a sign for Yucca Mountain first emerged.

"Planning a storage facility for nuclear waste that can last for approximately 10,000 years is one of the most pressing issues facing our country," the Department of Energy wrote in a letter in the nineties. "Therefore, because inadvertent intrusion into this nuclear waste repository might result in an accidental release of radioactivity, the Department of Energy is creating a panel to study the implementation of a marker system that could deter people from intruding on the repository for the next 10,000 years."

Dispatched in 404 copies, the Department of Energy's letter was delivered to seventy-seven linguists, sixty-six geologists, fifty anthropologists, forty-one astronomers, thirty-nine historians, twenty-nine biologists, twenty-eight psychologists, twenty-seven ethicists, fourteen graphic artists, thirteen science writers, ten archival specialists, seven print librarians, four sculptors, two painters, a mayor, and MENSA, and explained that

> "this panel will identify the effectiveness of marker systems throughout human history, and will then be asked to design several solutions for the problem at hand. . . . The knowledge that is necessary to develop such a marker will be significant indeed. We are therefore assembling a panel of experts that will be multidisciplinary in nature, spanning the fields of materials science, astronomy, climatology, the social sciences, and art. Each panel member will help with questions that directly relate to his or her expertise. . . . A materials scientist, for example, may help identify from which materials the marker should be made, . . . a linguist may be concerned with what kind of language should be employed, . . . [while] a landscape architect may help arrange the placement of the marker, . . . etc."

to which there responded fifteen geologists, fourteen engineers, thirteen linguists, eight astronomers, five anthropologists, four climatologists, four sociologists, three landscape architects, two historians, an ethicist, an archeologist, an artist, one wife of a famous dead cosmologist, the president of the League of American Women Voters, the executive director of the National Heart, Lung, and Blood Institute, and the secretary of the American Society for the Advancement of the Study of Petroglyphs.

In the end, the Department of Energy chose thirteen of those candidates, assembled them into a group that soon became known as the Expert Judgement Panel, and gave them each a check for $10,000, a deadline of two years, and the challenge to design the world's most important sign.

Before that group was ever assembled, however, the Department of Energy sought the advice of a man named Thomas Sebeok, America's leading expert in the field of semiotics, the study of how signs and symbols communicate their meanings.

In his report to the Department of Energy entitled *Communication Measures to Bridge Ten Millennia*, Sebeok explained that communication is a social function whose purpose is to ensure the continuity of society. It does this, he added, primarily through storytelling, something that can't exist outside a network of social systems.

Indeed, while Sebeok believed that the universe is in fact composed of signs, he also claimed that this doesn't guarantee that such signs are communicative. For while "communication" suggests an explicit understanding between a sender and a receiver, "signification" can exist without the intention of any message.

What Sebeok recommended for Yucca Mountain, therefore, was an active communicative system, one whose purpose and importance could be relayed and renewed throughout the future by messengers.

In his report, Sebeok suggested establishing "a long-term commission that would remain in service for the next ten millennia . . . self-selective in membership, independent of political currents, and licensed to use whatever devices for enforcement that may be at its disposal . . . including those of a folkloristic nature."

Sebeok called this commission The Atomic Priesthood, an international institution made up of 200 individuals whose responsibility it would be to maintain the knowledge that Yucca Mountain is dangerous, while also laying a trail of myths about the place in order to keep people away.

> "Each successive generation of The Atomic Priesthood would be charged with the responsibility of seeing to it that our behest is heeded by the general public—if not for legal reasons, then perhaps for moral ones—with the veiled threat that to ignore our mandate would be tantamount to inviting some sort of supernatural retribution."

These days, there are 297 individual companies that specialize in creating signs for casinos in Las Vegas. The city even boasts the only full-time accredited sign-making school.

And according to an industry magazine called *Signs of the Times*, Las Vegas is home to the "world's tallest sign," the "world's brightest sign," the "world's heaviest," "longest," "most famous," "most expensive," and even, says the editor, the world's "greatest" sign.

But long before experts started rating Vegas signs, merchants in the city understood their importance. In 1905, the year Las Vegas was founded, most buildings in the city were just wood-framed tents, but even then their canvas sides were covered with painted ads: *BUTCHER, HOTEL, GUNS, GIRLS.*

By 1930, when the population of Las Vegas was still under 5,000, the American Sign Company opened the city's first professional sign-making store:

IF YOU NEED A SIGN BAD . . . AND
YOU WANT IT GOOD, CALL US!

Back then, gambling halls were confined to a single city block. Their buildings were often just two floors high, but their signs could be as tall as five and a half stories.

Today, just the base footings of the average Las Vegas sign can require excavations almost two stories deep. They take 100 truckloads of concrete to anchor. Twenty-four thousand individual light bulbs. Forty-seven thousand feet of neon. A hundred fifty miles of electrical wiring. And an average construction cost of $13 million.

One morning, Sandra Harris, the executive director of

the Las Vegas Neon Sign Association, a private organization dedicated to preserving the city's oldest signs, took me on a tour of what she called the Las Vegas "neon boneyard," a full square block of outdoor storage with a wire fence around it.

"This is where signs used to go to die," Sandra explained as she pulled open the gate. "But not anymore."

Two women in bikinis and a man without a shirt leaned over and straddled a giant rusted X.

"Hey, guys!" Sandra said.

"Hey, girl!" yelled the models.

Sandra explained that the models were taking photographs for an ad.

"I think they've started a new business. A party-filling service."

Party-filling? I asked.

"Like if you want to get some buzz going for an opening you're having, you can hire these guys and they'll send over attractive people to mill around."

The two women stood in front of a giant red *O*, their breasts pushed together, their mouths opened wide.

We stepped into the lot.

There was *LADY* spelled in cursive against the boneyard's fence. There was a yellow and black *W* that was taller than me. A red and white bucket of Kentucky Fried Chicken lying on its side beside a *fleur-de-lis*.

Beside that was a *VACANCY*.

Beside that a *NO*.

There was a pink double *S* from Sassy Sally's Casino, *DEB-BIE* from Debbie Reynolds's, *NUGGET SINCE* from the Golden Nugget of 1979.

Also *GOLDEN NUGGET* from 1962.

GOLD from '48.

A piece of *D* from '16.

There was *OTEL* and *ASINO* and *OYAL* and *ARK*. There was *MECHANIC ON DUTY FREE ASPIRIN TENDER MERCY*. There was a bearded and bald leprechaun facedown on the ground, his arms sprawled in front of him with gold coins in each hand.

"That's Mr. Lucky," Sandra said.

"Can we shoot him?" asked a model.

"Can't," Sandra said. "Wish you could, but he's copy-righted."

I walked over to Mr. Lucky to sit beneath his shoulder's shadow. He was fiberglass and shiny and smelled a little like piss. I stood up and walked around him, looked behind him, climbed on top. In the area of Lucky's anus was a wide and jagged hole, inside of which were shirts and socks and a jar of Icy Hot. Underwear, a magazine, a basket of chili fries. In the winter, Sandra said, a homeless man lived in Mr. Lucky with a cat.

"Hope he's all right now," Sandra said. "I haven't seen him in a while."

"All cities communicate some sort of message," noted three art historians in *Learning from Las Vegas*, the first serious study of Las Vegas and its signs. "But in this city, the signs hit you immediately once you cross the Nevada border, and then they don't let up until you've reached the other side."

They're persistent, unsubtle, the most successful illustration of "full-immersion messaging":

> "Like when the facade of a casino becomes one big sign, or when the shape of a building reflects its name, and the sign, in turn, reflects the shape. Is the sign the build-ing, or the building the sign? These relationships, and the combinations between signs and their buildings, between architecture and symbolism, between form and meaning, are deeply relevant to the significance of this place. . . . These little low buildings, grey-brown like the desert, separate and stand out because of their signs. They are false fronts that engage as you pass them on the road. If you take away these signs, there is no Las Vegas."

The city, they concluded, is a sign.

"That's why I thought we should have a say in designing the marker for Yucca," explained the organizer of the Yucca Mountain Warning Sign Design Contest, an event Las Vegas held for amateur local artists. "I figured that if we had to live with this waste in our own backyard, we might as well try to help design the marker for it."

Inside the Harry Reid Center for Environmental Research on the campus of the University of Nevada, 300 people mingled on the exhibit's opening night. There was cheese, square crackers, red carbonated punch. There was a reporter from a local TV news station—*YOUR 24-HOUR UP-TO-THE-MINUTE LAS VEGAS NEWS SOURCE*—walking around with a mic in hand and a camera screwed into a tripod. There was a line leading to a curtained room with an "online conceptual model." There was a couple debating in front of "Shit," and then in front of "Phallus." There was the reminder, twice, by two guys in tank tops, that if I wanted to go to the afterparty it was "BYOB or forget it."

There were black cardigans, black berets, black eyeliner, dyed hair.

There was a short man in his twenties in a white diaper and bib.

"My design," explained the man, "is a performance piece about the childishness of this whole Yucca thing."

Indeed, the most popular designs at the exhibit that night tended almost exclusively toward the performatively rhetorical, those with titles such as "Bio/Mechanical Hazard," a proposal whose design was powered by the mountain's own waste—

> "At the core of my warning sign is a magnetic generator which creates a force field wrapping ten miles around the site so that any living creature that penetrates the field will create a disturbance that will produce an electromagnetic discouragement, a reminder of just how lethal this nuclear waste is"

—or "The Poppin' Fresh Universal Sign"—

"The Poppin' Fresh Universal Sign is an extremely large and durable plastic device based on the popular pop-up timer that's found in frozen turkeys. These devices are released when the internal temperature of a turkey reaches 183 degrees, which is the melting point of the metal that's used in the device. The metal melts, a spring's released, and the action signals to housewives that their families will soon be sitting down to a wonderful turkey meal. In much the same way, the Poppin' Fresh Universal Sign will let the future know when Yucca's waste is safe"

—or "Pull My Finger," a clear acrylic box on a white Corinthian pillar that was filled, according to the artist, with two weeks' worth of his own feces, a design that he equipped with a rubber orange finger that was connected to a tap—

"The only way to safeguard the future of our planet is to bury this nuclear waste under the only other substance more repugnant to humans. We need to create on top of Yucca a gigantic mound of our own human filth that will be so foul that any person who encounters the mountain will end up vomiting and shitting themselves in disgust, thus adding fresh odors to this self-sustaining system, and simultaneously scaring off any Yucca Mountain intruders"

—which, in demonstration, the artist pulled down.

"I wanted to leave my mark on Las Vegas," casino owner

Bob Stupak once said about his Stratosphere, the hotel that he constructed on the Las Vegas Strip, the single tallest American building west of the Mississippi. "What I wanted to do for Vegas is what the Eiffel Tower did for Paris, or what the Empire State Building did for New York. . . . I wanted my building to be a symbol, to be entwined with the meaning of Vegas."

"Well, yeah," said Dave Hickey, an art critic at the University of Nevada in Las Vegas. "He definitely created a new symbol for Las Vegas. But that still begs the question: what does this symbol mean?"

Dave Hickey has been called the city's resident art historian, an ambassador for Las Vegas to the rest of the world.

"You know why I like it here?" he said. "Because everything in this city is economically driven. And that's the only true democracy there is in the world. That's why I like teaching art students in Vegas. None of them are fucking wimps."

We met one morning before nine o'clock at a bar on the Strip called the Fireside Lounge, a room of red couches, octagonal tables, a neon strip of blue surrounding pit fires, and mirrors on every wall, floor-to-ceiling, wall-to-wall.

Three men in black suits were drunk on one couch, a couple on the next was making out with loud moans, a woman on another was alone with Bloody Mary, and Dave at the bar in black cowboy boots was funneling a free bowl of peanuts to his mouth.

"Sure," he said, "the Stratosphere's the tallest dick in Las

Vegas, that's true, and when you have the biggest dick you get some respect. But I also think the fact that the building is so fucking big is why it has had so much trouble in this town. Las Vegas architecture is all about commerce, and commerce is about flexibility. There's absolutely no gap here between a thought and an act. This city prides itself on its ability to follow the whims of tourism, because that way, if something doesn't work, you're more psychologically prepared to try something else. If you build something and it fails, you just blow it up. Buildings, neighborhoods, politicians . . . whatever. This city doesn't assume that anything's permanent. But the Stratosphere can only be exactly what it is. I mean, that thing's there to stay. And that's what's wrong with it. The Stratosphere's trapped being 'The Stratosphere' forever."

In 1996, only two years after the Stratosphere opened its doors, experts were consulted about how they might demolish it.

"That's a good question," said the Stratosphere's contractor.

While most buildings in Las Vegas are chicken wire, stucco, and steel support beams, the Stratosphere is composed of several hundred thousand cubic feet of concrete.

"Basically, you'd have to fell it like a giant tree," said Mark Loizeaux, an implosion expert who oversaw the demolition of the Stardust. "You'd incline it in one direction by tilting it explosively, and then you'd explode all the rest of it while it was falling to the ground. Basically, you'd want to turn the whole thing into gravel while it was still in midair, pieces the size of your living room couch. The biggest problem with doing that, though, is that you'd need to have an area to do this in that's as wide as the building is tall."

In other words, an area of land on the Las Vegas Strip that was a quarter-mile long, and vacant.

"Plus," he added, "there's the issue of cost, because you'd probably end up spending more to take this thing down than it actually cost to build."

Approximately a billion dollars.

"So I'd say it's there to stay," said Loizeaux.

"It's just not what people come to Vegas for," said Dave. "This isn't New York, this isn't Chicago, we're not a city of great buildings. We're the city of shtick and gimmick, the place that you come to when you need to escape."

From what?

"From what do you think?" said Dave.

He called a waitress over, asked for more peanuts.

"Look at the most successful hotels in this town," he said. "What do they got in common? They're all ceilings and floors and no fucking walls. Casino designers know that people don't like gambling with a lot of space above them. So when you look at a place like the Bellagio, which is the most successful hotel this city's ever seen, it's got this giant open floor plan of eighty thousand square feet, but it's all underneath a really low ceiling. It's multilayered, if you look at it. You've got the main ceiling above everything, and then that steps down to a lower level, and then there's a hood that hangs under that, and then an awning under that. So what you end up with is a twenty-foot-high ceiling that's got nine feet of headroom. Why? Because the hotel knows that the reason people come here is to be protected from God. I'm serious. No one's consciously thinking about this, but that's why they're here. They want as much space between them and Jesus Christ as they can get while they're fucking around. That's why hotels that emphasize their heights don't really do well here. I mean, you've got the Luxor, right, with its light that shoots into space. That opened up in the mid-nineties as a luxury hotel, but ten years later they've got some of the lowest room rates on the Strip. Rooms at the Paris Hotel are usually discounted too, despite the fact that it cost a billion dollars to build. That's because it's just not a welcoming place. It's got tons of tiny windows built into its facade that create a huge towering sense of height over the viewer. People don't want to be looking up while they're visiting this town, because no one comes here to pray. So if you put a fucking mountain in the middle of Las Vegas you're gonna have some fucking problems."

Initially, Bob Stupak wanted to build what he envisioned would be the tallest sign in the world. It would stand beside the low-rise facade of Bob Stupak's Vegas World, a twenty-story structure whose theme—"The Sky's the Limit"—was to be written vertically in neon up the length of a rocket ship that would stand 1,000 feet high. At that time, it would have been the tenth tallest structure on Earth.

"But around that time my daughter was living in Australia, and I went to visit her," he said. "We had lunch at the Sydney

Tower, which is a thousand feet high and has a revolving restaurant at its top. I saw people standing in line for an hour just to pay for a ride in an elevator to get to its observation deck. And I suddenly had an idea. I was only trying to build a sign in Las Vegas, but what if I put an observation deck on the top of my sign? People would come from all over the country just to stand up there and look. And then at some point I asked, 'Well, why can't it go higher?' Which is when I decided to make the sign 1,149 feet high, instead of just 1,000 feet high, because that seemed like a more scientific number. And then that's when the whole idea of building the world's tallest sign stopped being a concern, because we realized that that's what we were already doing. The very structure itself would be an advertisement."

Since 1993, the Stratosphere Hotel has received seven awards from the *Las Vegas Review-Journal*'s annual readers' poll, including "Ugliest Las Vegas Building," "Trashiest Place in Vegas," "Building Most Deserving of Being Imploded," and a special commendation for Bob Stupak himself: "Most Embarrassing Las Vegan."

There have also been eight fires at the Stratosphere Hotel, two of which occurred before the hotel even opened, and one of which broke out during its opening celebration.

There has been one guest strangled to death in his hotel room by strangers, a machine gun fired in the parking garage, and a lawsuit involving over 18,000 plaintiffs.

There was the Federal Aviation Administration's warning that the architect's plan for the 1,000-foot-high tower was 600 feet over airport regulations. And then there was the response from the mayor of Las Vegas that "it's [the FAA's] job to make planes safe for Vegas . . . it's not the other way around."

There was, for a long time, once construction on it began, the rumor of an anomaly that locals called a "kink," a bend in one of the tower's three 800-foot-high legs, which the Stratosphere's contractor assured city residents was not a significant structural defect, but which some months later, on an early desert morning, disappeared after it was spray-filled with Styrofoam and painted.

There was, before its opening, the hotel's stock price of $14.

And then, once it opened, its price of 2¢.

There was the $35 million that it was supposed to cost to build, the $500 million that it actually cost to build, and the $800 million that it accumulated in debt.

There was the hotel's bankruptcy.

There was the man from Utah who jumped off in 2000.

The man from Britain who jumped off after that.

The jump by the producer of *Las Vegas Elvis*, a local reality television show about one of the city's official Elvis Presley impersonators, who said to reporters, when he heard of the jump, "Now whenever I see it, the Stratosphere is going to be my heartbreak hotel."

There is its appearance from a schoolyard trampoline: alone in the sky on the long brown horizon.

There is its appearance from a nursing home window: alone in the sky above the treeline.

And when coming into the city on 95 from the north or 15 from the south or 93 from the east, there are the five or the sixteen or the twenty-one miles during which the Stratosphere stands alone in the distance, alone over the valley's high rim of black mountains, alone at the middle of the Las Vegas Strip, alone at the end of a bridge called Poet's Bridge, a few blocks from the tower, in a rough part of town, upon which someone has written with black Magic Marker—over the concrete verses that are inscribed on the bridge—*You wonder what you'll do when you reach the edge of the map, out there on the horizon, all that neon beckoning you in from the dark.*

HOW

The life span of black ink in disposable plastic pens is estimated to be about four and a half years. The blue ink in plastic pens starts to fade away in two. And newsprint is only intended to last for a day.

Already, scientists are experiencing difficulty in deciphering the technology that's used in Univac, the earliest working computer from the late 1960s.

And even the laser-encrypted plastic that we put on compact disks is likely to start peeling off in about forty years.

A color photograph, says Kodak, will last for thirty years. Videotape for fourteen. Magnetic tape, seven.

The life span of skywriting is about nine minutes.

The life span of a sunbeam is six.

And the light that reflects off the Moon every night is traveling so quickly that it only lasts a second.

"It's the medium's fault when communication fails," Vic Baker said in his laboratory office.

A geologist at the University of Arizona in Tucson, Vic served on the Department of Energy's Expert Judgement Panel, helping to design the marker for the nuclear waste repository.

"That's not a great surprise, though, is it?" asked Vic. "I mean, things decay. We know that. Nothing in this world is forever."

Vic was in a safari hat and sandals and white athletic socks, and as we spoke in his office one late fall morning he looked over my shoulder into a lamp without a shade.

"People have this really weird conception of science," he said. "They think that it's the one reliable source for information that we have. They think that even if their public leaders are not to be trusted, and their newspapers are inaccurate, and cultural and religious morals are treacherously shifting, that science, at the very least, will provide a stable compass. But the problem is that science can't do that. Science is alive, it evolves. It occasionally establishes a fact, but, if given enough time, it'll probably refute that fact. Remember when the Earth was flat? Remember when the Sun and all the other planets spun around the Earth? Remember when humans became sick because the gods were angry with us? Science just uses a kind of rhetoric that sounds authoritative. Just like any other form of communication, however, science is susceptible to abuse, inaccuracy, and just bad interpretation. And that's what's wrong with Yucca. The public wants to have some assurance that all this waste that we're producing is going to be safe in that mountain. So the Department of Energy creates all these computer models to try to prove that that's the case. They measure and measure and measure and measure till they get the results that they want. And then whammo: Surprise! Their computers predict that everything will turn out fine at Yucca Mountain. Phew!"

He pulled the left sock on his left foot up.

"Well, I'm sorry," said Vic. "I've got news for everybody. Our descendants are going to live in a reality in the future; they're not going to live in a computer simulation."

And then the other sock.

"The problem with wanting unwaveringly definitive results from science is that whenever we say we have an 'answer,' we also tend to believe that we've revealed some sort of 'truth.' But real scientists don't settle so firmly into answers. They always leave a little wiggle room for new evidence to change their minds. The very fact that we still even have something that's called 'geology' is an indication that we admit that we don't have all the answers. That we're still investigating."

In a report entitled *Durability of Marker Materials for Nuclear Waste Isolation Sites*, the American Society for Testing and Materials exposed a Lucite rod, a red brick, and a concrete block to the same conditions that they would face over 10,000 years at Yucca. After only ten simulated years of study, however, the Lucite rod was found to have already lost a third of an inch from its surface. The concrete block lost an inch and a half. And the clay of the red brick was worn away by two inches. So, in an environment like Yucca's, over a period of ten millennia, all three materials would eventually disappear.

The society broadened its study, therefore. It tried limestone mortar, a material that can be found in the buildings of Jericho, a city that's estimated to be 9,000 years old. In Yucca's windy environment, however, limestone would only last for a couple hundred years.

The society then tried lead, since lead is known for its exceedingly low levels of corrosion. But lead's softness was ultimately found to be too easily vandalized.

So stainless steel was then considered. But since stainless steel has only been in use since its invention in the late 1920s, its long-term durability is ultimately unknowable.

The society tried ceramic. But that lasted 1,000 years.

The society tried copper, which held out for 5,000.

How about granite? the society wondered. Granite samples have been shown on some mountain walls to retain the same polish they received from passing glaciers, tens of millions of years ago. But granite is also known to be extremely porous. In fact, in a study of one of the two giant obelisks known as Cleopatra's Needles, which were carved in ancient Egypt in 1500 BCE, almost an eighth of an inch was found to have worn away from the surface of one of the obelisks just twelve years after being transported to London. If Yucca Mountain's climate were to change over time, and if precipitation rises in the region as is expected, a granite marker would eventually pit, crack, and fall completely apart.

After three years of study, the society concluded that the most durable materials that could be used at Yucca Mountain would also be among the most expensive in the world: titanium, sapphire, and something called "Synroc."

"Metals such as titanium and sapphire have too much value to human culture, however," the society noted in its study. "A marker that is constructed out of either of these would most likely be looted by intruders."

Synroc, on the other hand, is an artificial compound that is made from three other relatively worthless substances— hollandite, zirconolite, and perovskite—materials that are reported to have survived for as much as 2 million years in a variety of simulated environments. When combined as Synroc, they can resist temperatures as low as 1,300 degrees below zero and 2,300 above. The American Society for Testing and Materials called this substance "the hardest stuff on Earth." And just a couple years after it was developed in Australia, Synroc was named by the World Nuclear Association "the single most promising material with which to handle most forms of high-level radioactive waste."

In fact, Synroc has become so promising that some countries are investigating whether it can be used as a container for their waste, essentially doing away with the problem of disposal by immobilizing the waste in inert chunks of Synroc.

This is an idea that was first proposed by the Department of Energy back in 1950. At that time, there were 6 million gallons of nuclear waste left over from the production of the first atomic bombs. The department's idea was to pour the contaminated waste into a molten mixture of a synthetic compound they called "borosilicate." The two materials would then be mixed until they bonded, hardened, stabilized, and eventually became indissoluble, flame-resistant, and virtually indestructible.

"We are on the threshold of the future," wrote the Department of Energy in 1950 about their waste solution.

But then, in '51, the Cold War began.

Defense spending in the United States increased by 60 percent, and the $5.4 trillion that was eventually spent in America on developing nuclear weapons—about 6 percent of the nation's entire GDP—included no budget whatsoever for nuclear waste storage.

So fifty years after first studying and abandoning one compound to immobilize our nation's nuclear waste, the Department of Energy found itself with a report from the American Society for Testing and Materials in which Synroc was now recommended for use at Yucca Mountain, but not as a substance for containing Yucca's waste—for which England and Australia and Japan and Pakistan and Russia and China and France are testing it—but rather as a medium on which to write our nation's message about this problem that we never found a real solution for.

"This is a project about faith," said the anthropologist David Givens, another member of the Department of Energy's Expert Judgement Panel. "I mean, it's a project about having faith that we can even pull this off. But it's also a project that requires faith to even think this would be necessary.

These days, a lot of scientists are predicting that the human race won't survive beyond the next few centuries. So there's something touching about the U.S. government making the assumption that it's crucial we warn our descendants about the dangers of nuclear waste. They're assuming that we'll have descendants."

David was in Tacoma, and I was out of the country, and so we spoke by way of a satellite relay.

"Hello?" David said.

"Hello?" I responded.

"Have you ever played that game they call 'Telephone'?" he asked. "You know, you whisper something into the ear of the person sitting next to you, and then that person whispers what you said to the person sitting next to them, and then that person whispers what they heard, and so on, and so on? It ends with the last person down the line finally revealing what they heard, which ideally would be the same thing that the very first person said, but of course it never is. There's always something that happens in the transmission of the message. People mishear things, so the message gets garbled. Or they can't hear all of it, so they make stuff up. Sometimes there's just some jerk who decides to change the message for the hell of it. The point is, in a situation like that, the message has to rely on the diligence and goodwill of its carriers. And this project is no different. What we're all talking about is a species-wide game of Telephone that's going to last for the next ten millennia. So, yeah, there's some faith involved. We're gonna have to trust each other."

"But the best thing to rely on in a project like this," explained Louis Narens, a cognitive scientist who was also on the panel, "is not some emotional connection that we imagine we have with the future, but rather the cognitive skills that are inherent in all of us. It's our intelligence that unites our species."

Louis has been teaching for a quarter of a century at the Institute for Mathematical and Behavioral Sciences at the University of California in Irvine. His publications have titles like *Ultra-Uncertainty Tradeoff Structures* and *Homeomorphism Types of Generalized Metric Spaces* and *A General Theory of Ratio Salability with Remarks About the Measurement-Theoretic Concept of Meaningfulness*, but when we met one sunny morning at his home by the beach there was a Labrador standing beside him at the door and his wife blending smoothies in a yellow jogging bra.

"Some people on the panel wanted to take an emotional approach to designing this sign, and I understand that motivation," he said, "because emotions are dramatic. Their impact is immediate, and they feel very deep. But the problem is that emotions are unreliable, too. An aesthetic approach to designing this marker would ultimately be irresponsible because nobody's really proven that emotions are universal."

Cognitive science is the study of how humans know themselves. It explores how we perceive, reason, and interact with the world through the complex negotiation of objects and ideas.

Its primary focus, rooted in the linguistic theories of

Noam Chomsky from the late 1950s, is that which makes the human mind unique in the world: its ability to represent things through the use of abstract signs.

"Language itself was developed out of signs," Louis said. "Five thousand years ago, small cuneiform notches were made on clay vessels in order to tell people how many sheep a person owned, or how many sheaves of wheat they owed somebody else. Inside the vessels were a corresponding number of tokens in the shape of sheep or wheat. Eventually, though, people realized that the tokens inside those vessels weren't really necessary as long as the notches on the outside of the vessels were acknowledged to be a counterpart to actual sheep or wheat. They were symbols, in other words. And this is what helped pave the way for representational language, allowing those notches to stand in for greater and greater abstractions. Not 'sheep,' for example, but 'goods.' And then not 'goods,' but 'property.' This is the beginning of cuneiform, the origin of written language. And it's when our species began to think about thought itself."

He wiped off a smoothie mustache.

"It's tricky, though," he said. "Because how far can we take the significance of a symbol? Jung would have us believe that what unifies human consciousness is the existence of emotional archetypes, generalized subconscious stimuli that affect all humans exactly the same way. As a cognitive scientist, however, I'm not so sure about that. I mean, as attractive as the idea of emotional archetypes is, their existence can't be proven. Lots of people have tried testing for the existence of archetypes by asking subjects to look at three different pictures and then to choose which of them express the same emotion. But do you know what happens? It doesn't work. There's never been any evidence from these studies that proves we 'feel' things in universal ways, because there's never any consistency in what people choose. And that makes sense, because this kind of test is really just an exercise in interpretion."

According to administrators of the Thematic Appreception Test, a psychological evaluation developed in 1935, "the human imagination in an individual mind is more unique than even a fingerprint." In the test, subjects are shown thirty-one individual images and then asked to compose stories to accompany each. As the test's originators once explained, the test is based on "the well recognized fact that when someone attempts to interpret something complex he is apt to tell as much about himself as he is about the matter he is trying to interpret. At such times, the subject is off his guard, since he believes that he is merely explaining objective occurrences. To a trained professional, however, he is exposing inner forces, wishes, fears, and traces of past traumas."

By 1943, the Thematic Apperception Test was said to have eclipsed the Rorschach Test in popularity among psychologists. Within another decade, it evolved into a series of specialized tests for "adult male subjects" or "adult female subjects" or "boys," "girls," "Negro Americans," "the handicapped," "the elderly," "veterans of foreign wars."

It was, as two psychologists claimed in the 1960s, "modern psychology's reigning personality assessment."

However, in a controversial 1999 study entitled "The Thematic Apperception Test: A Paradise of Psychodynamics," the Thematic Apperception Test was administered to a twenty-five-year-old subject dubbed "John Doe." Following the test's protocol, John was asked to view the thirty-one standard images and then to compose a story that could accompany each. In response to an image of a boy who is sitting alone while looking at a violin, John wrote:

> "This child is sick in bed. He has been given sheet music to study, but instead of music he has come across a novel that interests him more. It is probably an adventure story. He evidently does not fear the possibility that his parents will find him thusly occupied as he seems quite at ease. He seems to be quite a studious type and perhaps regrets missing school, but he still seems quite occupied with the adventure in the story. The adventure in the story has something to do with oceans. He is not too happy, not too sad. His eyes are somewhat blank, the result of reading a book without any eyes. He disregards the music and falls asleep with the book."

The administrator then invited thirty-one of the world's preeminent psychologists to review what John had written, the results of which—

> "Quite likely he is a member of some minority group"
> "He is probably a mainstream All-American boy"

"He was very clearly overprotected while growing up"

"Feels neglected by the world"

"Fears social disapproval"

"Lacks positive personal relationships"

"Is afraid of his father"

"Sees his father as inadequate"

"He may have had an excessive number of premature sexual affairs"

"He has never had an authentic sexual experience"

"He has had homosexual relationships out of desperation rather than desire"

"His Oedipal problems are not yet resolved"

"I see no significant damage"

"There is little hope for recovery"

"Seems fatalistically resigned to the rejection of the world"

"Has an ingrained hopeless pessimism"

"Seems hopeful for the future"

". . . a dominant drive for security"

". . . an enormous amount of hostility"

". . . a great deal of love to share"

". . . a decreasing ability to distinguish between fantasy and reality"

". . . an exceptional imagination at work"

". . . a pathological loosening of an orderly thought process"

". . . seems to be in the early stages of paranoid schizophrenia"

". . . the depression is so powerful that suicide could be likely"

". . . I think he is very creative"

—were described in a review in the *Journal of the American Medical Association* as "probably the most profound psychological dissection ever performed on a single human."

"We all interpret differently," Louis repeated. "But the point is that the more complex we make our message, the more likely it is that a future civilization will be able to decipher it correctly, because a complex message will leave less room for vagueness and more opportunities to countercheck our intentions. It can't be just a shorthand message for 'danger,' in other words, or a picture of a stick figure entering a mountain with a big X drawn over it. It has to be something that's multilayered, a mixture of different communicative media that people in the future will have to work through in order to understand its overall meaning, using the natural functions of the cognitive mind. In short, we have to give these people a problem to solve. We can't just give them the answer. And part of that strategy will have to involve using language effectively."

"Yeah," said Fritz Newmeyer, a linguist at the University of Washington in Seattle, "except languages have the unfortunate habit of regularly failing."

Red-haired and slim and bearded-to-a-point, Fritz met me on his campus at the student union center. He bought a banana and a cup of coffee and said, "You've got an hour."

Fritz described himself as the "maverick" on the panel.

"I was alienated from other members of the group," he explained, "because I was really outspoken. I thought this whole project was bullshit from the start."

In his field, Fritz is best known for compiling a four-volume study on the history of modern linguistics, a discipline that tracks the roots, uses, and transformations of the world's many languages, as well as their demise.

"I have a set of the *Encyclopaedia Britannica* from 1911," he said, "and every now and then I like to look at it just to see what kinds of changes our culture has experienced. There's Latin and Greek in this edition, for example, and the Latin and Greek aren't translated. But these days, of course, everything in the *Britannica* would be translated for us. So obviously this tells us a lot about the differences between the encyclopedia's readership in 1911 and its readership today. It tells us, for example, that Latin and Greek aren't considered integral to our educations anymore. And this not only suggests something about the amount of social change that we've experienced since 1911, but it also says something about the changes that those two languages have undergone. Latin and Greek are now the domain of scholars, or of those who might have attended private schools where these languages are still taught. Nevertheless, there has been some change to both these languages and to our culture. Does this mean our culture is going to hell, as we tend to say when change occurs? Or does it just mean that our culture has evolved, and thus so have our needs for language? My point is that a language either changes to better suit its culture, or it atrophies, just like everything else. And then it eventually dies."

Linguists estimate that there are currently 6,700 languages in use around the world, half of which will disappear within the next century. Among these, only about 100 are spoken by 90 percent of the world's inhabitants, leaving the fates of the remaining 6,600 languages to just 10 percent of the population.

"So the problem that we faced on the panel," Fritz explained, "was that even if we worked with the world's strongest languages, there was still no guarantee that any of them would last, because languages naturally fall out of use. For example, say we left a message that was written in English, and it was simple and straightforward and incredibly precise. What do you think are the chances that someone in ten thousand years will still be able to read it? How many people even speak English today?"

"I don't know," I said. "Maybe about thirty percent?"

"Thirty percent of what?" Fritz said.

"Of the world."

He put down his banana.

"How many people live in the United States?" asked Fritz. "Plus in England, in Australia, in Canada, South Africa, New Zealand, Ireland, Scotland, etc.? How many people in all these cultures? How many of them can speak and read English fluently?"

"Okay," I said. "Thirty-five percent?"

He stared.

I looked down.

"Let me give you a hint," he said. "It's not thirty percent and it's not higher than that."

"Twenty?" I said.

Fritz closed his eyes.

"Fifteen? Ten?"

"Stop," he said. "It's five percent. Okay? Just five percent of the world's population knows how to read or speak English. That's all. And only fifteen percent speak Mandarin, which is the world's most popular language. So nobody's got a majority. And that's my point. This is a project that's attempting to accomplish what can't be done, which is communicate in a way that will be coherent to anyone on the planet at any given time between now and ten millennia from now. We have never been able to do that. And we probably never will. So what we really ought to do is invent a language that can be universally understood."

In 1941, American linguist Morris Swadesh began devising a system to help him more efficiently trace the roots of languages in order to determine how quickly they'd evolved from their original sources. In linguistics, the most common reason for doing this is to better understand the cultural influences that have affected a language over time. The less obvious reason for doing it, however, is to pursue what some linguists like to call the ultimate "mother tongue," a single root for every language, but a root that some linguists don't even believe existed.

Swadesh, working in exile in an underfunded lab at the

National School of Anthropology in Mexico City, believed
that an easier way to pursue his research than conducting
expensive firsthand fieldwork would be to construct a template of basic vocabulary with which to compare a variety of
languages, thus achieving a quick survey of languages' inter-
relatedness. While most languages change dramatically over
time, Swadesh theorized that a basic set of vocabulary was not
only likely to exist in every world language, but that such a
basic vocabulary would also be more likely to resist significant change, because fundamental words serve essential roles
in human culture. The vocabulary list that Swadesh created
was made up of words that describe body functions, natural
phenomena, sensory experiences, and physical dimensions.
He developed a list of 200 such words—

all, animal, ashes, back, bark, belly, berry, big, bird,
bite, black, blood, bone, breast, breathe, brother, burn,
child, claw, clothing, cloud, cold, come, cook, count,
cry, day, die, dig, dirty, dog, drink, dry, dull, dust, ear,
earth, eat, egg, eight, eye, fall, fat, father, fear, feather,
fight, fire, fish, five, float, flower, fly, fog, foot, four,
full, freeze, give, good, grass, green, guts, hair, hand,
he, head, hear, heart, heavy, here, hold, horn, how, hundred, hunt, husband, I, ice, if, kill, knee, know, lake,
last, laugh, leaf, left, leg, lie, live, liver, long, louse, man,
many, meat, moon, mother, mountain, mouth, name,
near, neck, new, night, nine, nose, not, old, one, other,
play, pull, push, raid, rain, red, right, river, road, root,

rope, rub, salt, sand, say, scratch, sea, see, seed, seven, sew, sharp, shoot, short, sing, sister, sit, six, skin, sky, sleep, small, smell, smoke, smooth, snake, snow, speak, spit, split, squeeze, stab, stand, star, stick, stone, straight, sun, swell, swim, tail, ten, that, there, they, thick, thin, think, three, throw, tie, tongue, tooth, tree, turn, two, walk, warm, wash, water, we, wet, what, when, where, white, who, wide, wife, wind, wing, wipe, woman, woods, warm, work, year, and yellow

—and called it the "Swadesh List."

By comparing the different versions of this basic vocabulary in any two languages, Swadesh believed that he could determine how closely related those two languages were, and thus how recently they had diverged from a common root.

In his book *The Origin and Diversification of Language*, Swadesh proposed that his technique could be used to trace human languages back 200,000 years, roughly 95 percent farther than with conventional techniques.

"If we can show by means of comparative linguistics that various peoples spoke similar languages sometime in the past," he wrote, "we can infer the identities of those predecessor languages, and thus even more intimate connections between all human cultures . . . arriving eventually at an original tongue."

Swadesh came to believe so strongly in the potential of his method that he began to call it "glottochronology," comparing it to the precision of radiocarbon dating.

"But the problem," Fritz explained, "is that he made too many assumptions. And that's the basic problem with any 'universal language.' In order for Swadesh's theory to pan out, every language would need to change at exactly the same rate. But just like two societies that exist across the globe from one another, languages evolve at vastly different paces. It just isn't possible to prescribe a universal rate of decay for every world language and then plug that into a formula to determine their origins. It's more complicated than that. There's really no way of determining what happened to a language over the past ten thousand years because we don't have any languages that have lasted that long. So how are we supposed to predict what'll happen to a language ten thousand years from now?"

"This is not a place of honor," reads a warning that was drafted by the Expert Judgement Panel, a message that is written in simple declarative sentences in an attempt to improve linguistically its chances for survival.

> "No esteemed deed is commemorated here. Nothing of value is buried here. This place is a message, and part of a system of messages. Pay attention. We are serious. Sending this message was significant for us. Ours was considered an important culture."

Fritz grabbed a napkin from a basket on the table. Did some math. Made a graph. Leaned across the peel of the banana splayed between us.

"What's the likelihood that this message will make it to the other side?"

As Fritz explained, if Modern English—the language in which Shakespeare wrote—is generally thought to be comprehensible to the average American high school student, and if Middle English—in which Chaucer wrote—is generally thought to be comprehensible to American college students, and if Old English—in which *Beowulf* was written, about a thousand years ago—is usually comprehensible to English scholars only, then it's likely that the use of contemporary English in the warning marker's message would appear to average readers a thousand years from now—

> "Nis weorðful stow. Nis last mære dæde na. Her nis naht geweorðes bebyrged. Þeos stow bið ærend ond dæl ærendworuldes. Giemaþ wel! We sindon eornost! þeos ærendgiefu wæs niedmicel us. Hit þuhte us þæt we wæron formicel cynn"

—as illegible as Old English appears to average readers today. And even its translation to those same average readers—

> "This is not an honorable place. It is not the marker of a glorious deed. Here is nothing at all of worth buried. This place is a message and a portion of a message-world. Pay attention well. We are earnest. This message-giving was great for us. It seemed to us that we were a very great people"

—would probably seem at best like an innocuous threat.

As Fritz explained, we tend to lose one word out of every five over the course of a millennium in English, a rate of decay that averages out to about 20 percent. Over the span of ten millennia, however, that rate of decay would increase to a loss of 89 percent.

So, by the end of the warning marker's life span at Yucca, the English in the message would only have retained 11 percent of its significance, and therefore of its meaning, and therefore of its ability—

"

    This

of

                          message

              world.

                                 This

          us

              were

                       "

—to say anything at all.

WHY

It's estimated that only 40 percent of suicides are the result of chemical imbalance, while the remaining 60 percent are caused by "undetermined" factors.

We know that people are ten times more likely to kill themselves in a city than other kinds of environments.

We also know, however, that rural can be bad.

As are the hours between noon and six.

Or May.

Or winter.

Or if you don't drink coffee your chances of suicide are three times higher than if you did.

Ditto if you are a woman who uses the pill instead of a diaphragm, are a man with tattoos on his neck or lower arms, are a child with green eyes, have any silver fillings.

If you were born under the signs of Aries, Gemini, or Leo: that is bad.

You are more likely to want to kill yourself during a new moon than a full one. More if you don't have pets, more if you own a gun, more if you earn between $32,000 and $58,000 a year.

More if you're male.

More if you're white.

More if you're over sixty-five.

It helps if you live anywhere in the United States other than Nevada, Wyoming, Alaska, or Montana, although the experts so far can't figure out why.

Nor have they figured out why Native Americans once tended to kill themselves more often than any other group, but then, fifteen years ago, stopped killing themselves significantly.

They do not know why, generally speaking, white suicide victims tend to shoot themselves, while black suicide victims tend to poison themselves, Hispanics tend to hang themselves, and teens to cut themselves.

Recently, Dr. John Fildes of the University of Nevada's College of Medicine received $1.5 million from the federal government in order to study the issue of suicide in Las Vegas, which is why, after the death of that boy at the Stratosphere Hotel, his office was the first I called for information about local suicides.

By the time I finally met Dr. Fildes in person, however, our appointment had been rescheduled four times in eight months, his federal grant had long expired, and all that we had learned about this problem in Las Vegas is that it still is a very big problem.

It was to Sergeant Tirso Dominguez, therefore, an officer at the Las Vegas Metropolitan Police Department's Office of Public Information, that I turned for information about Las Vegas suicides. But "I don't want to be a part of anything like that," was how Sergeant Dominguez responded to my request for information.

It was from *Reporting on Suicide: Recommendations for the Media and Public Officials*, a pamphlet of guidelines developed by the Centers for Disease Control, that I learned that " 'no comment' is not a productive response to media requests for information about local suicides."

It was Eric Darensburg, assignments editor at KLAS Channel 8 in Las Vegas, who told me that his station had a policy against recording footage of suicide scenes when I asked to see the footage that his station had recorded of the scene outside the Stratosphere on the evening that boy died. And it was Eric Darensburg who also said, when I provided him with the date on which his station aired that footage, that their film librarian was out of town, that their library was currently very messy, that he wasn't going to be able to track any footage down.

It was from Bob Gerye, principal of the Las Vegas Academy of International Studies and Performing and Visual Arts, where that boy was a student for two years before he died, that I received no comment in response to my request for his insights about the effect of suicide on his school. But it was Bob Gerye who did say, in response to the teachers and parents and students who requested that a memorial be held at their school, "No."

And it was an eyewitness to that death at the Stratosphere Hotel—a man who'd made a statement to the police about that night, plus several informal statements to various TV stations, one online local blogger, and a weekly tabloid paper—who said to me, "Fuck off," when I asked him for a comment.

"This," said the man, "is a private matter."

Yet more people kill themselves in Las Vegas every year than any other place in America.

They kill themselves in Las Vegas so often, in fact, that you have a better chance of killing yourself if you live in Las Vegas than you do of being killed there, despite the fact that Vegas is one of the most dangerous places in which to live, according to the FBI's *Uniform Crime Report*. In Las Vegas, more people kill themselves than die in car accidents, die of AIDS, die of pneumonia, cirrhosis, or diabetes. Statistically speaking, the only things more likely to kill you in Las Vegas are heart disease, stroke, and a few types of cancer.

Otherwise, in Las Vegas, you're going to kill yourself.

Maybe this is why the city also has the highest number of smokers per capita in the country. Or the highest rate of drug use among teenagers in the country. The highest number of American arrests for driving under the influence.

The highest high school dropout rate.

Highest household bankruptcy rate.

And the highest number of divorces nationwide, every year.

According to the executive director of Westcare, the city's only full-time mental health care facility, an average of 500 residents seek psychiatric treatment every month in Vegas, but an estimated 49 percent of them never receive that treatment. Indeed, in a nation in which an average of thirty-three hospital beds out of every 100,000 are typically devoted to psychiatric care, Las Vegas devotes just four out of 100,000 beds to mental illness.

Some speculate that this shortage of treatment for local mental illness has contributed to spikes in the city's homelessness. According to a 2000 report in the *Las Vegas Sun*, the homeless rate in Las Vegas quadrupled in the nineties—from 2,000 people in 1989 to 8,000 people in 1999—an increase that motivated voters in Las Vegas to pass new "quality of life" laws through which dozens of downtown sweeps have since been conducted, citing "jaywalking, sidewalk obstructing, and other violations as an excuse to arrest homeless residents and clean up problem areas," thus leading the National Coalition for the Homeless to call Las Vegas in 2003 "the meanest city in America."

And yet *Time* magazine has named Las Vegas "The New All-American City."

Retirement Places Rated said it's "the nation's most desirable retirement community."

And *Fortune* magazine called Las Vegas "the best all-around city in the United States," the same year in which a study entitled *Social Stress in the U.S.* ranked Las Vegas the single most stressful city in which to live.

"The only real problem Las Vegas faces," said cultural critic Hal Rothman, chair of the Department of History at the University of Nevada, "is people like you who come from other places who don't know shit about this town but want to write about it."

The "people like you" to whom Rothman was speaking when he said this were fifteen young journalists from Berkeley, California, who had come to Las Vegas, as Rothman suspected, in order to write a series of essays about the place, a project that resulted in a book entitled *The Real Las Vegas: Life Beyond the Strip*, a collection of hard-hitting cultural criticism that has since been called one of the most insightful portraits of the city since *Learning from Las Vegas*. It was published around the same time as Rothman's own study, *Neon Metropolis: How Las Vegas Shed Its Stigma to Become the First City of the Twenty-first Century*, a book of conspicuously aggressive boosterism for a work of supposed criticism, a combination of cultural pandering and pro-business rallying from an author who seems never to have met a corporate shark he didn't like.

Indeed, that "shit about this town" which Rothman insists only locals like himself are allowed to write is seldom actually written about by Las Vegas locals.

"Another sign of how much America's fastest growing city has become hostage to the corporate lords of gambling," Sally Denton and Roger Morris wrote in a December 2000 article in the *Columbia Journalism Review*. "This situation seems borne out by the number of local reporters who, like elected politicians and public officials, tend to end up on the public relations staffs of Las Vegas casinos."

In 1983, for example, when Las Vegas casino owner Steve Wynn decided to apply for a gaming license in Britain, *The Independent* of London reported that an investigation by Scotland Yard drew links between Wynn and the Genovese crime family, an investigation that subsequently was referred to in advertisements by the publisher of a new book about Steve Wynn, *Running Scared: The Life and Treacherous Times of Las Vegas Casino King Steve Wynn*. However, even though *The Independent*'s report was never challenged, Wynn still sued the publisher of *Running Scared* for what he considered "libelous statements," winning $3 million in a Nevada state court, bankrupting the publisher of the biography in question, and somehow winning support from Las Vegas journalists, such that the allegations that initiated his suit were covered by the daily *Las Vegas Review-Journal*—arguably the most influential paper in the state—for only one day, in only one article, on page 5, section B, under the quarter-inch-high headline "Wynn Sues Local Writer."

In contrast, the *Las Vegas Review-Journal* provided several weeks' worth of coverage for Las Vegas mayor Oscar Goodman when he sued a writer named Jim McManus, an Illinois reporter whose popular memoir, *Positively Fifth Street*, alleged the mayor's participation in planning the assassination of a local judge:

"With Jimmy Chagra on trial in Texas for heroin traf-
ficking, Jack, Ted, and Benny Binion convened in booth
no. 1 of the Horseshoe Coffee Shop with Oscar Goodman, the hyperaggressive young attorney representing
the accused. The upshot of that meeting was a $50,000
contract for Charles Harrelson, actor Woody's father,
to assassinate U.S. District Judge John Wood—or so
the lore has had it."

That "lore" surrounding Las Vegas mayor Oscar Goodman
has always had it that actor Woody's father was indeed once
hired, that Judge John Wood was indeed once murdered,
that Mayor Oscar Goodman did indeed defend Chagra, and
indeed that his defense of those figures in Las Vegas whom
residents widely recognize as members of the mob were the
kind of close relationships that helped get Goodman elected,
but that meeting at the Horseshoe as described by McManus
could not be proven as anything but "lore," which is why,
as the *Las Vegas Review-Journal* wrote about his suit, "the
Mayor took offense at this besmirching of his name," and
which is why, as the *Las Vegas Review-Journal* also later wrote,
"Mayor Oscar Goodman may have defended reputed mob-
sters, but that doesn't mean he is one," and which is why, as
the *Las Vegas Review-Journal* also later wrote, "ironies abound
in Mayor Goodman's life, for here is a man who fiercely
defends his acquaintance with casino Black Book members
and crime family capos . . . and here also is a man who
demands respect," and which is why, as the *Las Vegas Review-*

Journal finally explained, "not only was the allegation that Goodman was included in a criminal conspiracy without factual basis, it wasn't the only error in that paragraph of the book. The dominant subject of that paragraph, Jimmy Chagra, was called a heroin trafficker . . . but in reality Chagra only worked with cocaine."

In the end, this was local coverage that so triumphantly succeeded for Mayor Oscar Goodman that within a few weeks, in the *New York Times Book Review*, a full-page ad appeared with a letter of apology addressed to Mayor Goodman, signed by the publisher of McManus's book. It was accompanied by a photograph featuring Mayor Goodman, arms folded, face smiling, legs spread and firmly braced beneath the shiny glass hull of the Stratosphere Hotel.

"We don't want anything in our city that might upset the tourist," state senator Dina Titus has said about her district, the 7th precinct of Clark County, Las Vegas, Nevada. "So if it's a touch of reality that isn't pretty, then we want to get rid of it. You don't want to come in contact with reality when you're here for a fantasy."

This is perhaps why, back in 1995, the Nevada Motion Picture Division refused the request of director Mike Figgis to film his Oscar-winning movie *Leaving Las Vegas* within the city's limits. The film depicts an alcoholic executive from Los Angeles who moves to Las Vegas to drink himself to death.

"No one wanted to be associated with that kind of script," the president of the Nevada Motion Picture Division said, the same president who granted permission for the filming of *Casino*, Martin Scorsese's movie about the mob in Las Vegas, and the same president who gave permission for the filming of *Showgirls*, a movie about the underworld of Las Vegas prostitution.

"Well of course people are paranoid about suicide here," Ron Flud explained in the County Coroner's Office. "I mean, it's in business, it needs tourists. Every resident's bread and butter is based on this city's image. And suicide doesn't sell."

Indeed, Ron Flud was the only official in greater Las Vegas who agreed to talk about suicide.

"I'm a finder of facts," he said, "that's my job, it's what I do. I don't see the point of concealing information."

The Coroner's Office in Las Vegas is tan and stuccoed and flat-roofed and small and wedged within a district of attorneys' offices and accountants' offices and psychiatrists' offices and banks. Inside it are no blood-spotted sheets covering bodies in the lobby or tumblers lying around full of cloudy yellow liquids, no people in the hallways wearing black rubber aprons or walking to and fro wielding shiny silver tools. In fact, the only indications that his office is responsible for determining the cause of death of everyone in Vegas is a small sign in the lobby—ATTENTION FUNERAL DIRECTORS—a plaque from Nellis Air Force Base—IN GRATITUDE FOR YOUR SERVICE—and someone's remark to a secretary as he passed her in a rush—"Thank you for the chocolate coffin, Pam."

"I think everyone's a lot more comfortable," Ron said, "if we keep a low profile here. Suicide is the most threatening thing that we can encounter as a culture. It's a manifestation of doubt, the ultimate unknowable. A suicide by someone we know—or even by someone we don't know—is an ugly reminder that none of us has the answers. So apply that to a city with the nation's most frequent suicides and you might start to understand this city's reluctance to talk about it."

In the year 533, at the second Council of Orléans, Catholic cardinals actually voted to "outlaw" suicide.

The Talmud forbids even mourning its victims.

And before one can ponder Islam's ancient question— "What ought one think of suicide?"—the Koran quickly answers: "It is much worse than homicide."

Hindus condemn it, the Buddha always forbade it, and in Zurich there was an ordinance once on the city's books that condemned all suicides to burials beneath a mountain.

"So that their souls," read the law, "may eternally be suppressed."

Psychologists were still debating the criminality of suicide as late as the 1970s, claiming that women who kill themselves after committing adultery—or, in the professional terminology of the time, "morally fallen women"—will usually commit suicide by jumping from a window. That gay men who feel ashamed of being "sexually penetrated" will stab themselves repeatedly until they are dead. Or that anyone who is maddened by "poisonous thoughts" will likely succumb to gas.

"I'd say the taboo surrounding suicide is the number one reason I get sued," Ron said.

Earlier in the week, Ron had been in court for a trial in

which a suicide victim's family had sued him to change his classification of their only daughter's death.

"Apparently, when I called it a suicide I prevented her from going to heaven."

He scratched his beard and looked away.

"And I understand their motivation, as silly as it seems. The whole cultural psychology of this city is obsessed with convincing ourselves that this is a place of leisure, that no one can get hurt here. But this is a city just like any other city. We don't live in the hotels, we don't eat dinner at the buffets, our wives and daughters aren't all feather dancers at lounges on the Strip. Las Vegas is our home. And it can be wild and it can be fun, but it's also a place with more suicides than anywhere else in America. Now, obviously I understand why the city doesn't include that in any of its brochures, but my point is that we can't fix the problem if we don't actually acknowledge it."

Behind Ron Flud in his downtown office was a portrait of George Washington mounted on a horse. A thin brown folder was on his wide, polished desk. Inside it, the cause of that boy's death at the Stratosphere Hotel—"multiple head and body traumas"—typed into the box that was labeled *BODY* in his three-page coroner's report.

"Anyway," Ron said. "Guess we should move on to why you're really here."

He opened and closed the folder intermittently as we talked, massaging out of it facts before then molding them into stories.

He said, for example, after glancing at a photograph of that boy's body after falling, that the worst damage done to a body in a fall is "internal, not external . . . believe it or not."

He said, "Did you know there's a maximum air speed our bodies will reach, no matter how high we jump from or how heavy we are?"

He told me a story about a woman in New Zealand who fell out of an airplane on a flight over mountains.

"She fell twenty thousand feet into a pile of snow, and she survived without major damage."

But he did not say that afternoon in his office, even after I asked him two or three times, whether it is likely that one would lose consciousness in a fall, such as that one from Stratosphere.

He did not say, as Albert Heim once did, a nineteenth-century geologist who studied mountain climbers, that "there is no anxiety, no trace of despair, no pain, no regret, nor any sadness as one falls from great mountain heights. . . . Instead, the person who is falling often hears beautiful music while surrounded by a superbly blue heaven that is filled with roseate clouds . . . and then, suddenly, and pain-lessly, all sensations are extinguished immediately from the body at the exact moment that the body makes contact with the ground."

In other words, Ron Flud did not explain how it was that this boy's sneakers in the Polaroid he showed me, lying twenty feet on the brick pavement from his body, were knocked off at the moment that his body hit the ground, even though his sneakers look unscuffed in the photo, unstained, still laced, and even double-knotted.

I suppose Ron knew that there are facts that do not matter.

"Okay, kids," Blair said, when our bus came to a stop. "I want you to show your school identifications to the soldier."

We were stopped at the southeastern guard gate of the Nevada Test Site, the checkpoint for entering the Yucca Mountain project. The Test Site encompasses 1,300 square miles of rocky Nevada desert, just a small portion of the 87 percent of the state that the federal government owns. It's on the Test Site where 900 nuclear weapons were tested between 1951 and 1992, where 129 of them were detonated above ground, and where the National Cancer Institute has subsequently determined that enough radioactive iodine has gradually been released to cause 75,000 cases of latent thyroid cancer.

GUNS ARE PROHIBITED, read a sign inside the gate. Also, *PETS*.

The guard who approached our bus was tall and bereted and flak-vested and armed, and as he walked he kept his machine gun erect in front of him.

"D'Agata?" asked the guard, when he stepped onto the bus.

"John D'Agata," he repeated.

"John, that's you," whispered Blair.

I raised my hand.

"Here."

"You're on another bus, sir, come with me," said the guard.

"They're my ride back to Vegas, though. Are you sure?" I asked.

"Another bus," said the guard, then waited for me to move.

I grabbed my bag.

Stood.

"Dude," said a boy, as I walked past him up the aisle, "they're taking that guy away."

Outside, a second guard opened an idling Jeep's door.

"I'm really only supposed to be going to Yucca," I explained.

The other got in the Jeep.

The driver started it up.

We pulled away from the bus and then went suddenly into desert.

During the nuclear testing that was conducted on the site, scientists made experiments in which chickens were blown up.

Horses, monkeys, pigeons, rats.

Cows were fed contaminated grass in experiments.

Bank vaults were built, and then they were bombed.

Whole railroad bridges, and then they were bombed.

Wood and stucco houses were built and then furnished, iceboxes stocked, bookshelves completed.

They sat mannequins in living rooms to enjoy a quiet evening.

Father in his chair, Mother on the couch, two kids on the floor pushing a ball back and forth.

After the bombing tests, clothes were removed from the mannequins and tested.

What kinds of fabrics should be worn in an attack?

Polyester stuck to skin. Cotton burned off it.

Patterned fabrics attracted light, while white reflected it.

In a nuclear attack, the testers concluded, wear white cotton clothes in a concrete house and your chances for survival improve.

There is a bowling alley still on the grounds of the site. A movie theater, steakhouse, post office, bank. A row of twenty newspaper vending machines that haven't been restocked since 1994, the year we signed the Comprehensive Test Ban Treaty and sent most of the employees of the Test Site home.

Just south of there, however, between the Yucca Mountain project and the city of Las Vegas, the Natural Resources Defense Council has reported that one of America's seven National Nuclear Stockpiles contains the fourth largest concentration of warheads in the world. Fourteen hundred missiles await decommission there, ten miles away from downtown Las Vegas.

"We have glorified gambling, divorce, and other doubtful pursuits—all in an effort to secure a national reputation," wrote the *Las Vegas Review-Journal*'s founding editor about the site, months before its opening in the early 1950s. "But now we can be part of the most important work being done by the United States federal government. We have found our reason for existence."

The Las Vegas Chamber of Commerce did its part during this time by distributing free twelve-month color calendars inscribed with the schedule of the site's atomic tests.

The Atomic View Motel would boast "the best views of the blasts from anywhere in Vegas!"

At the Sands they held an annual "Miss Atomic Bomb" pageant.

And at a women's hair salon inside the Flamingo they lifted women's coifs into a bundled-up creation that they called without irony "the mushroom 'do."

In the late 1950s, Elvis Presley appeared in Vegas as the "Atomic Singing Kid," and when he later returned in the 1970s for his comeback tour, marquees were still billing him as the "Atomic Entertainer."

Later, in the nineties, Miss Nevada praised the state's long heritage with the bomb in a local news report entitled "Miss Nevada, Newly Crowned, Supports Yucca Mountain."

And even during the summer that we first moved there, just weeks before the U.S. Senate would vote on Yucca Mountain, 250 people in the state of Nevada petitioned their legislators for a new novelty license plate that featured a mushroom cloud.

As we drove toward the mountain in the white Jeep that day, two black jets in the distance sped by. They swept low against the desert. Then each dropped a bomb.

"Fuck yeah," said a guard as we paralleled the explosions.

"Fuckin' A," said the other.

A fascination with how the world will end is not particularly new.

God initiated this obsession of ours when he explained to us in Genesis that everyone would be killed by a single giant flood.

Roman prophecy said it'd happen in 600 BCE, the year in which Romulus was told in a dream that his empire would be destroyed.

It will happen before I die, said Confucius to his pupils.

It will happen twenty-nine times, said the Sibyl throughout her life.

Four hundred eighty-three times, St. Clement later revised.

In 968, there was a solar eclipse.

In 981, Halley's Comet appeared.

New Year's Eve brought the end in 999.

Then the plague brought the end in 1346.

Brought the end again in 1349. Thirteen sixty-five. Seventy-one. Ninety-six.

On pain of death, said the Vatican's Fifth Lateran Council of 1516, there shall be no more predictions of the end of the world. ·

But the planets aligned in Pisces in 1517, so the end of the world was predicted by way of flood again.

The young American prophet Jacob Zimmerman predicted the end in 1674, the year in which he led a group of men into the forest, christening them "The Society of Women in the Wilderness." Mary Bateman's magical chicken in Providence, Rhode Island, predicted that the end would come in 1813. John Wesley, the founder of Methodism, concluded that chapter 12, verse 14 in Revelation—"the time, times, and half a time"—meant that the world was going to end in 1836.

In 1910, a group of thirty-one adults in Oklahoma City sacrificed a ten-year-old girl to stop the end.

In 1938, during *War of the Worlds*, the end was heard live on CBS Radio.

In 1948, with the establishment of Israel.

In 1954, according to Charles Manson.

When Atlantis reemerged in 1968, Gulf Stream currents dramatically were altered, thus producing a string of tsunamis worldwide, then hurricanes, then earthquakes, and then the end of the world, as predicted by Edgar Cayce.

On September 21, 1982, the Trinity Broadcasting Network canceled its regularly scheduled programs in order to air a full day of instructional videos about Armageddon's approach.

And on October 28, 1992, the end was predicted by sixteen-year-old Korean prophet Bang-Ik Ha, who claimed that "50 million people will die in earthquakes," "50 million people will die in traffic accidents," "50 million people will die from fire," and "50 million people will be crushed by falling buildings"—an announcement that caused 5,000 people to quit their jobs in South Korea, eight to kill themselves, and one to seek an abortion the day before the end because she feared she'd be too heavy for God to raise to heaven.

I guess it made some sense, therefore, that during the same summer when a decision of such destruction would be made about Las Vegas, 250 locals would sign up to have a mushroom cloud license plate printed.

By then, a study by the RAND Center for Terrorism Risk Management entitled *Considering the Effects of a Catastrophic*

Attack named the local Vegas stockpile of 1,400 warheads "a primary domestic target in a nuclear attack."

Perhaps those 250 residents had already figured out that in the event of such a strike on that stockpile of warheads, ten miles away from downtown Las Vegas, the resulting blast would only take a millionth of one second. It would expand into a fireball ten miles across. It would travel at 758 miles per hour, and its temperature, according to *The Effects of Nuclear Weapons*, a 1979 study by the Department of Defense, would be "five times hotter than the sun."

And so perhaps those 250 residents had already assumed that if the temperature of the Sun is, as *The Effects of Nuclear Weapons* estimates it is, about 25 million degrees Fahrenheit, and if five times that amount is 125 million degrees Fahrenheit, and if the temperature at which a human body combusts is 1,600 degrees Fahrenheit, and if such a blast of heat would reach their bodies, ten miles away from the site of detonation, in approximately four and a half millionths of one second, and if pain impulses in the human body are believed to travel 382 feet per second, and if all of this is shorter than the time it takes to climb by elevator or to climb by foot or to climb inside one's own private mind above the city's lights—looking down at them from the stratosphere for one final view—then it is more than likely that in the event of a nuclear strike on the nearby National Stockpile, just a few miles away from anyone in Vegas, the minds of most Las Vegas residents in the path of that blast would literally not know that they were being destroyed until sixteen hundredths of one second afterward.

"All right, sir," said a guard, when the Jeep came to a stop. "They're meeting you inside. Say you're here for Yucca Mountain."

I entered a large building that was the same brown as the earth.

Inside a man named Wally said, "Hi, John, I'm Wally Lee."

He handed me a badge and then he asked me what I thought.

"Is this Yucca?" I asked.

"Not yet," Wally said.

I followed him outside to a dark waiting van.

"Wally," I asked, "did I do something wrong?"

"No, no," Wally said. "I've got you going with the press. Better tour, that's all."

"But I'm not with the press," I said.

"Oh, yeah? What's your project?"

"I'm not really sure."

"No problem," Wally said. "That's just what we call this tour."

Inside the van were three young congressional aides. There was a professional blogger. There was a famous chef. There was a man with a plan to build the city an indoor ski resort. There was a man from *Time*, one from the *Post*, and a photographer from the Associated Press.

We drove with Wally seven miles further into desert, north a couple miles and then east a couple miles and with no one saying anything until *Time* asked, "No guards?"

"Nothing yet to guard," Wally said.

So we drove.

A high pile of brown rock eventually emerged. It was labeled with a white sign posted on a stake: "Caliche #1." We turned right and bent around it and saw another pile staked— "Caliche #2"—then a third one, a fourth, and then finally in white outposts as large as the rocky piles there were six plastic tents with domes and metal frames. The tents had names like "Lab F," "Workshop," "Medic Treatment Storage."

Wally stopped the van beside a tent without a sign and said, "Everybody out. Here we are. Leave your bags."

"What about our notebooks?" asked the *Post*.

"No notebooks," Wally said. "We'll give you notebooks inside."

Inside the tent brown mud was splattered up the plastic walls. A sound like something metal being forced into a mold. There was a Good Humor ice cream novelty machine.

Also Pepsi.

Cappuccino.

Nuts and candy.

Hot broth.

Wally said, "Okay," then called us over to a closet. He handed us each a yellow hat, earplugs, safety goggles, orange vest, lamp.

"Now this," Wally said, "is a personal self-rescuer," a rubber mask and metal tank that lashed around our waists and that Wally demonstrated how to wear in case of fire.

"The mountain is basically a very long cave," Wally said,

"so in a flash fire everything is going to burn very quickly. If you put on the self-rescuer, you'll be able to breathe through the smoke for a little bit of time."

"How much time?" someone asked.

"Three minutes," Wally said.

The tank, he explained, converts carbon monoxide into carbon dioxide through a chemical reaction that will occur in our mouths.

"It's going to burn like hot coffee being poured down your throat, but that's how you know it's working, so don't get freaked out."

"Carbon dioxide isn't safe to breathe, though," someone said.

"Little bit," Wally said.

We walked outside.

Maybe noon.

There were machines not in sight doing something to each other, a low idling hum underneath them in the air, yellow dust, yellow hats, 99 and 105 and higher in degrees.

"What about our notebooks?" someone asked.

"Oh, yeah," Wally said, then turned and yelled to a man in the cage of a machine. "We got any more notebooks?"

I don't know, shrugged the man.

"No more notebooks," Wally said.

We walked single-file past a "Hospital" white tent, a large piece of plywood leaned against its plastic side. We walked around it. Rubbed our eyes. We passed a group of men who stared and stood and ate their lunch. There was a horn that was sounded. But there was no reaction. There was a sound coming from someone up ahead within our line. Our heads watched the ground and the mountain bits of litter. There was a small rectangular bulge in the back pocket of *Time*. Someone said, "I'm hungry." Someone else behind was coughing. There was a brightness attached to everything and then exposing it too long.

"Goggles on!" Wally yelled as we came up against a wall.

"Earplugs now!" Wally yelled.

"Okay, lamps!" Wally yelled.

Beside us was a rocky wall and inside it was a hole. Twenty feet in length and very black within its center. Around the hole were spots of brown which Wally said was natural. He called it "desert varnish," the substance Anasazi carved to make their petroglyphs.

Now around the hole were just long stripes of indentations, the holes that had been drilled to blast away the mountain's rock.

Rail lines ran inside the hole and quickly disappeared. Three black cables hung above until they disappeared. A long accordion silver tube beside them disappearing.

"This is Yucca," someone said.

"This is Yucca?" someone said.

The mountain coughed up gusts of tiny granite shavings.

"Get on!" Walled yelled when we reached the mountain's hole, climbing onto a tram with five benches on the rails.

I sat beside *Time*. He sat beside the *Post*.

"Hold on!" Wally yelled as he honked us through the hole.

The three congressional aides in front of us yelled, "*Wee!*"

We were traveling through the mountain at seven miles per hour, maybe five miles per hour, past alcoves to the sides of us that were lined with black fencing, some bolts attached in patterns to hold back the Yucca rock. Above us was more fencing and some concrete spackled patches.

We passed "Exploratory Studies Lab" in alcove number three, an underground facility in which a two-year study tested what would happen if Yucca Mountain were ever struck by tidal waves.

Wally stopped the tram. Said "something" "something" "water" "water."

This mountain looks dry, it's not, he said, *wet . . . safe . . . like trying to dissolve your toilet in* "something" "something" "water" "water."

Two aides looked at Wally, then each other, raised their hands. "Something" "something," one aide said.

Absolutely, Wally said.

We moved on.

Wee!

I asked *Time* if he could hear. He pointed to something nodding, it was blackness on the wall.

We passed "Drift Scale Heater Test" in alcove number nine, a lab in which a vent was heating rocks inside of Yucca to 384 degrees Fahrenheit. *Imagine,* Wally said, *your home heating bill!*

One aide started laughing.

We moved forward.

Someone, *Wee!*

We passed more lunchers eating, passed stoplights on the blink, passed NO VISITORS BEYOND THIS POINT and then beyond that point: we passed a three-mile stretch of nothing as the tram sped up and heads flipped back and the lamps on all our helmets swished small circles on the walls, the back of Wally's head, someone's white and wide-eyed face, the walls where blackness happened, and then *Time* at blackness, *Post* at blackness, cufflinked aide at watch and then at friend and then at blackness. *We're going down!* yelled the guy from the desert ski resort. We were either going down or very quickly going straight. One aide turned and pointed at some blackness on the wall. *Time* quickly nodded at him and then pointed up ahead. I looked over, then at him.

I still saw only black.

When I started to volunteer that summer at the Las Vegas Suicide Prevention Center, what I thought it would do is give me something to say about Yucca Mountain.

"Some people say it's drugs, and others say it's stress, and of course there are always people who blame our suicides on the gambling," explained Marjorie Westin, the director of the center. "But I've been studying this city's problem for my entire adult life and none of those theories are right. The truth is that there isn't any answer to this problem."

Marjorie Westin founded the Las Vegas Suicide Prevention Center when she was a still a graduate student, thirty-five years ago. There are twenty-three people who volunteer for the center, one of whom is on duty at any given time, receiving calls in his or her own private home. This is a

variation on the standard hotline procedure in which two
hotline counselors usually answer calls together, providing
each other support in a centralized location. But given the
volume of calls that the hotline receives, plus the dearth of
volunteers who are available to work, the Las Vegas Suicide Prevention Center employs a local answering service
to screen its calls first, then to forward the important ones
to a volunteer on duty.

"I wish we had the luxury of an office," said Marjorie.
"And if we had the right funding and enough volunteers, of
course I would prefer that we have a whole team of people
helping each other out every evening on the hotline. But
every year, without fail, there are three hundred suicides in
the city of Las Vegas. That's one every twenty-six hours. So
if I've got twenty-three volunteers taking six-hour shifts, well
. . . you do the math. We're fighting a losing battle."

In comparison, the Suicide Crisis Call Line upstate in
Reno is a twenty-four-hour center with a rotating staff of
sixty-five volunteers, each of whom receives fifty-six hours
of professional training, and all of whom are certified by the
American Association of Suicidology.

"Some people assume the Reno center is better than ours,"
said Marjorie. "But their hotline is in a city of four hundred
thousand people, and every year their budget is a hundred
thousand dollars. Las Vegas has a population almost five times
that size, and a suicide rate that's six times higher. The most
I ever get in funding is fifteen thousand dollars. So Reno's
hotline isn't better than ours. It's Reno itself that's better.
Theirs is a city that cares."

One night, toward the end of the city's centennial celebrations, my mom and I attended a cake-cutting downtown. It was hosted by Sara Lee in an indoor sports arena, and it featured what was advertised as "the largest birthday cake in the history of the world!"

"All weekend people have been coming up and asking me, 'Mayor, why have you built such a big birthday cake?'" the mayor was heard recounting for reporters in the arena. "And you know what I tell them? I say that it has to be this big, it has to be the best, the greatest, the most exciting cake that anyone's ever made. Because that's what Vegas is! This whole cake is very symbolic of our city."

It was seven layers high and the size of a basketball court.

It came on seven refrigerated semitrucks in 30,242 pieces. In 18,000 pounds of sugar, 24,000 pounds of flour, 135,000 eggs. An estimated 91 million calories.

At midnight, those of us who had marched in the Centennial Parade were asked to gather around to watch the mayor cut the cake. I counted eight other people who had marched in the parade. Plus my mother. Dignitaries. Maybe another 200. Maybe 250.

We cut the cake and then some volunteers passed it out.

It was good. A yellow pound. The frosting was very sweet.

There weren't any plates so we had to use cardboard. Then there wasn't cardboard so we had to use our hands.

There was enough cake, someone said, for everyone in Vegas.

"That's the real reason it's so big," said the president of

Sara Lee. "We wanted to make sure that everyone had a chance to taste the cake, because it's their birthday, too. And we all know that it's bad luck not to eat your birthday cake!"

At the end of the night, only 5 percent of the cake had been consumed.

Instead of distributing the leftovers to nursing homes and local schools and homeless shelters, though, the birthday party organizers arranged to have it bulldozed, then driven fourteen miles to a ranch outside of town where sixty-seven pigs were corralled to finish it.

That summer, after the Senate's vote approving the Yucca Mountain project, after documents leaked by workers at the Yucca Mountain project showed proof that scientists were falsifying their studies, after my mom moved out of Summerlin to a studio apartment when the job she went to Vegas for disappeared within three months, and after a spate of suicides convinced the County Coroner that the local suicide record would be broken yet again, reports began to appear about strange fish at Lake Mead: genetically mutated, physically deformed, their spines twisted in knots and the females all infertile.

It turned out that in its haste to divert more water for its growing population, Las Vegas had built its pipeline only six miles downstream from where it also dumps its waste, risking what biologists were calling that summer "the beginning of the extinction of human beings in Las Vegas."

During my training as a hotline volunteer, I learned about what Marjorie called "the perfect hotline call":

"The best call," she said, "will result in five answers to these five basic questions.

"First of all, who are they? Obviously, the reason you want to know who they are is so that you can use their name to help them feel more comfortable while you're talking to them.

"Then, what are they planning on doing? Do they just want to chat, or do they have a gun in their hand?

"Where are they? Are they home, in their car, in a public place? We have a lot of hotels here in Las Vegas, so 'How to Handle Calls from the Major Hotels' is the chapter in our manual that will help you deal with that.

"When are they going to do this? There's a difference, of course, between someone who's having a bad day, and someone who's just swallowed a whole bottle of Seconal.

"And that brings us to 'How.' We've talked about guns and we've talked about pills, but of course there are many other ways that we can kill ourselves. There's suffocation, there's cutting, there's hanging, immolation . . ."

"What about 'why'?" I asked during class.

"No," Marjorie said. "We don't ask 'why.'"

"Why not?" I asked.

"Because 'why' is what gets asked in therapy with a counselor. It's not something we can handle on our hotline, hon. We're here to offer information to our callers, like where to find a therapist so they can get themselves

some help. But asking 'why' opens up a whole new can
of worms. And trust me, it gets messy. You don't want
to deal with 'why.' "

"I have often wondered why," wrote suicidal artist Edvard
Munch in his journal, "the art I'm most attracted to is that
which has been painted with someone's own blood."

Born the oldest son in a family of five, Munch created
his best known work before he turned twenty-nine. By that
time, his mother had died of tuberculosis, and his father had
also died. Munch's older sister had died as well, and so had his
younger brother. By the time he finished *The Scream* in 1893,
the only remaining member of Edvard Munch's family was
committed to an asylum for "unnatural nervousness."

It was a time when child slavery was legal in Norway.
When young women were sold to brothels that were sanc-
tioned by the state. When four out of nine workers at Nor-
wegian matchstick factories could expect to lose an average
of two fingers on the job.

"I was walking along the road with two good friends
one day," he wrote. "The sun had just gone down, the
evening coming slowly. I felt a heavy weight of sudden sadness in the sky: it had become a seething red.
I stopped, leaned against a railing that was bordering
the harbor, and looked out at the flaming clouds that
were hanging there like swords, their blood-red blades

reflected in the water. My friends had already passed. But I was frozen there. A loud and piercing scream was shaking through the air."

It was once described by Carl Jung as "man at the shoreline of reason and doubt." It was once described by Jackson Pollock as "the destruction of every painting that had ever come before it." And it was once described by Edvard Munch as "I live with the dead every day."

A cardboard sheet two feet by three, wax pastel scores of red and yellow and green, a boat mast clipping the long horizon like a cross, the sea too blue with current, the infected spinning sky, and against the wooden railing looking at us, but not out, a small and frightened figure whose expression we might recognize from William Blake's drawing of his angel Uriel, standing guard at Eden's gate and shrieking at intruders.

We can see it in the sculptured gasp of Bernini's black *Damnata*.

Caravaggio's *Medusa*.

Masaccio's *Expulsion*.

In the grip he feels before he dies in *Laocoön and His Sons*.

It is there when Arnold Schoenberg's nameless woman screams at nothing.

When Clytemnestra in Strauss's opera screams for three full metered measures.

When Hamlet finds Ophelia, Othello Desdemona, or the wind catches up with Macbeth.

It was there in Darwin too, at the nineteenth century's end, when he announced in his study called *The Expression of Emotions in Man and Other Animals* that "all human emotions can be easily diagnosed" for they are "instincts that we can trace back to our cells and nothing else," a theory that diffused all unknowing from that painting, any sadness, any doubt, any lingering threats of wonder, such that now a century after Darwin's revelation we are able to sell the painting as a plastic blow-up doll—

"Work! Kids! Taxes! Deadlines! Politics! Diets! Mondays! Arrgh! When you can't make life any better, make it funnier . . . with the Giant Scream Inflatable!"

—or in commercials for General Motors' new Pontiac Grand Am—

"This car drives like an absolute scream!" says an animated version of the painting's frightened figure

—or in print ads for M&M's new dark chocolate candy treats, featuring a cartoon M&M playing hopscotch in *The Scream*—

"Dark just got fun!"

"Why do you feel like the world is going to come to an end?" I asked a hotline caller my first night of volunteering.

"Because it isn't going to come to a beginning."

I was home, at my mom's, taking the calls that the answering service forwarded to my cell.

We had the television on.

The cat was on her back.

My mom was beading jewelry to make some extra cash.

One man called to masturbate while he whispered, "I'm so lonely."

A lot of people hung up after silence or just breathing.

One woman called while crying during the local evening news, screaming at me "Whore!" when the weather forecast started.

I sat that night with the manual for six hours on my lap, sometimes opened up to the chapter DO'S AND DON'TS—"Don't ever dare a caller to 'go ahead and do it'"—and sometimes to the chapter on SUICIDE FACTS AND FABLES—"suicide is believed to be contagious among teens"—and sometimes to the chapter on USEFUL INFORMATION— "if somebody's calling you, they probably want your help"—but I could never figure out which information I should use, how much talking I should do, how much listening, be how friendly, exactly how much to feel.

What I never figured out while volunteering all that summer is what it was I thought I was doing as a hotline volunteer.

I do not know how to fix a problem if that problem is someone's solution.

People would call the hotline and I would start to understand. Instead of saying, "no," "you're overreacting," "every-thing will be fine," I would sit sometimes and nod, forgetting that there were answers I was supposed to have to give.

I do not think that Yucca Mountain is a solution or a problem. I think that what I believe is that the mountain is where we are, it's what we now have come to—a place that we have studied more thoroughly at this point than any other parcel of land in the world—and yet still it remains unknown, revealing only the fragility of our capacity to know.

But as each new caller reached the line, instinctively I reached out to grab that hotline manual, its lists of things to do, a bag of Swedish Fish, my mother for a stick with an orange feather on it, and my mother's cat, with just her eyes, for some movement in the air.

It was Saturday and hot and the wind was blowing hard but did not come in the house.

The moon began to show up. Only half of it arrived.

A young boy called briefly, didn't say very much.

And then my shift continued on through *Hitler and the Occult* and *Trading Spaces: Boston* and the local late-night news, on which a white and mottled sheet was shown rumpled on the ground. Blue lights. Someone's shoes. The red pavilion entry of the Stratosphere Hotel, around which a perimeter with yellow tape was drawn.

WHY

"The reason why we scream," explained Aaron Sell, a fellow at the Center for Evolutionary Psychology, a research center at the University of California at Santa Barbara, "is because we need someone's help. It's really as simple as that. It's an instinct that we developed hundreds of thousands of years ago before we had any language, and it's so simple a call that is so deeply ingrained in us that we can understand the meaning of a scream from anyone."

His research primarily explores the phenomenon of "instinct blindness," our tendency to take for granted our impulse for survival.

"Other animals share the same impulse, of course, but we're the only ones with the ability to ask why we possess this impulse," he said. "And yet, we seldom ask 'why?' It's odd that when it comes to this very fundamental question, we usually just avoid it, or we assume we know the answer. Why do we protect ourselves? Why is screaming instinctual? Well, among most mammals it's also an instinct of altruism. Those animals that tend to have a lot of kin, and who tend to live with those offspring, also happen to be the ones who make a lot of noise."

Reptiles, explained Aaron, rarely say anything. That's because most reptile species are solitary, seldom raising their offspring. East African vervet monkeys, on the other hand, live in massive families, and they've not only evolved the ability to make a lot of noise, but they've also developed several dozen variations of screaming.

"They have a specific scream for snakes," said Aaron. "And in experiments, if you play it for them, they'll jump into the trees to try to get out of danger. But when they hear the scream for birds, they scamper down and try to hide closer to the ground. They even have a special scream that's specifically pitched for rain in order to better penetrate the acoustics of moist air."

And humans aren't very different.

"We conducted a study with a tribe of people in Bolivia called the Tsimane," Aaron said. "We asked them to scream a variety of statements in their native language, and then we played those screams for undergraduates here in Santa Barbara. Now, even though none of these students had any idea what the Tsimane were actually saying, about sixty-five percent of them were still able to understand the general gist of those screams. And that's especially impressive considering how few of us in the U.S. live in the kinds of environments in which understanding the subtle differences between screams is necessary. We can still do this, though, because screaming is one of those traits that we developed as a very primitive species. It's inherent in all of us."

Over the past couple decades, however, our cultural use for screaming has dramatically evolved. These days, self-defense experts advise people to yell "Fire!" if they ever find themselves in danger. They specifically advise us *not* to scream. According to the producers of *Just Yell Fire*, a popular self-defense video aimed at teenage girls, most people don't want to get involved with helping a stranger unless they think their own safety is also being threatened.

"Culturally speaking," said Aaron, "this makes the biological instinct to scream ineffectual in modern life."

Aaron's field is an approach to psychology that believes that the human mind is a network of data-processing machines that were designed by natural selection hundreds of thousands of years ago. The purpose of these machines, according to this theory, is to solve the problems that were faced by our earliest ancestors. They weren't developed, in other words, to solve the problems of today.

"We have equipment all over our bodies that don't serve useful functions," explained Michael Karnell, the director of Otolaryngology at the University of Iowa. "I mean, at one point they served a function, but we've since evolved away from needing what they do."

The appendix is notoriously superfluous, for example.

So are some of our teeth.

Or the remnants of our tails.

"In my field," Michael said, "it's a part of the voice box that has become superfluous. Every larynx is composed of a series of vocal folds that close over airwaves to vibrate when we speak. That's the useful part of the box. But each of us also has a whole other set of vocal folds that are called the 'false folds,' because they don't really do anything. They're really only used when we need to scream. Now, of course, there are always some people who find a use for these folds. Heavy metal singers, for example, can sometimes train their false folds to help them produce a kind of guttural rattle. But for the rest of us, these folds just sit there most of the time. They're a very good example of how the human body hasn't biologically kept up with the cultural evolution of the species."

This is because natural selection, says Leda Cosmides, the founder of the study of evolutionary psychology, takes a long time to respond effectively to environmental change.

The time it takes to build brain circuits that are suited to particular societal needs is as slow as the time it takes for wind and sand to sculpt and smooth a stone.

"Even relatively simple changes can take tens of thousands of years," she's written. "And yet, the computer age is only a little older than the average college student. The industrial revolution happened 200 years ago. And agriculture appeared on Earth just 9,000 years before that. So our species has only spent about 1 percent of its existence living in any kind of

modern world—roughly one-millionth of the time that we
spent living as hunters and gatherers. . . . So there just haven't
been enough generations of us yet to allow natural selection
to design the right brain circuits for the world we're living
in. Our modern skulls still house a fundamentally Stone Age
mind."

"But even though it's no longer the most efficient instinct
to have," said Aaron, "screaming is still likely to happen when
we find ourselves in need. You can't fight biology. The body
knows when it's in danger, and it's going to do what it has to
do in order to survive."

And yet, according to a study by the University of Chicago,
only 39 percent of Americans believe that we'll even survive
this century. In another 10,000 years, Vega, not Polaris, will
be our North Star. The space satellite Voyager, which was
launched in 1979, and which has since been traveling 40,000
miles per hour, will be closer to the absolute emptiness of
space than it will be to our home. Even the Earth's continents,
which have been migrating slowly since they initially were
formed, will be 850 feet farther apart.

There will also be a new axial tilt in our planet. It will
temporarily shift us away from the Sun, lowering global temperatures by as much as 50 degrees.

Around Yucca at that time there will be a grassy plain. Most
of Russia won't be inhabitable. Iran will be a ski resort.

A new volcanic island will appear beside Hawaii.

Plastic will be extinct because petroleum will be too.

And while we won't be living longer than we currently are

living, Frank Tipler's book *The Physics of Immortality* says that
if we're wealthy we'll be able to buy the brains of younger
body donors, download our memories into their minds, and
then live through them vicariously until we need another
donor.

We will be living underground. Or we will be living in
giant domes. Or we will be living in a single networked city
that sprawls across the planet called "Ecumenopolis."

Physicist John Fremlin believes, in fact, that the human
population by the year 12,000 will be 61 trillion strong. Our
food will have to be harvested from algae and cadavers and
pumped into our homes as daily liquid rations.

Rodney Brooks, the director of MIT's Artificial Intelligence Laboratory, believes however that humans are going
to have such exquisite control over the genetics of living
systems that instead of growing a tree, cutting it down, and
then building a table from it, we ultimately will be able to
just grow a table from scratch.

Yet as Warwick Collins explains in his book *Computer
One*, most of the work on the planet by the late twenty-first
century will be conducted by a giant global supercomputer
that will relegate humans to the role of pampered pets. It
will control the water supply, the food supply, electricity,
transportation. It will be programmed to repair itself and to
anticipate situations that might necessitate more repairs, and
this is the reason why, 500 years after we invest in building it,
Computer One will calculate the chances that human beings
might interfere with the work it's programmed to do. It will

reason that interferences are a threat to its efficiency. And it will logically conclude that it could raise its productivity if humans were not around.

It will be quiet on the Earth.

There will be a lot of wind.

From the ridgeline of Yucca Mountain we might look down at "Black Hole," one of the designs for a warning marker from the Expert Judgement Panel. Ninety thousand square feet of black basalt stone irregularly carved and cobbled onto the sandy ground.

"A crazy-quilt of parched land," the panel describes it as. "Cracked, hard to walk on, projecting the image of nothing, a void, uselessness, a place that would seem unwelcoming and uninhabitable because the region will absorb so much heat through these stones that an intruder will simply not be able to stand being there."

Or we might stand on Yucca Mountain and listen to "The Moans," an echoing aural effect from a series of stone sculptures that would be carved to emit a single pitch in the wind.

"A minor D," writes the panel, "because that note usually signals to our brains that it is sad."

They will fill Yucca's basin with a mournful constant cry, scaring off intruders through an effect that some theorize can be supported by biology, since "pitch extraction from music is accomplished in the inferior colliculus of the brain, which itself is situated in close proximity to other midbrain centers known to be part of mammalian reward systems," according to a study by neuroscientist Martin Braun entitled "Inferior Colliculus as Candidate for Pitch Extraction." "The pitches found in major chords may therefore have a direct or indirect influence on these reward nuclei, which could be one of the reasons why music can have so strong an emotional impact, and why major chords are regarded as joyful and minor chords as mournful."

Or we may see "Forbidding Blocks." Or we may see "Rubble Landscape." We may see "Irregular Grid," "Spikes in a Field," "Landscape of Thorns," "Tall Leaning Stones." We may see a whole catalogue of visceral warning markers, artificially built environments we'll be meant to enter into to help make their warnings work.

But these will be environments, writes the panel in its report, "that will exist without transmitting any gestalt for the intruder," "without perceivable foci," "without the possibility of being understood."

Why?

We must find ourselves, the panel says, having an experience: an essaying into the purpose of what's apparently purposeless, an essaying that tries desperately to cull significance from the place, but an essaying, says the panel, that must ultimately fail.

"All human cultures," writes the panel in its report, "have tried marking spaces that they have wanted to call 'the center.' It is an impulse to create order out of the chaos that surrounds us: the tribal fire, the village temple, the city's clock tower. But this is why we must invert the symbolic logic of this site, establish a sense of meaninglessness around the entire mountain, suggest that there is no single place of value at the site . . . that the land itself is shunned . . . devastated by the Earth."

But what we are likely to see instead, according to recent reports from the Department of Energy, is a small series of twenty-foot-high monuments at the site. They'll be carved in the shape of pyramids and made from local granite. On their surfaces will be inscriptions in English about the site, plus the date the waste was buried, the date it will be safe, and a small engraved image in the apex of each stone that reproduces the anguished face from Edvard Munch's *The Scream*.

"It's the most recognizable painting in the world," said a Department of Energy spokesman when I called to ask about it. "Human culture will probably change dramatically over the next ten thousand years, but human emotions won't. So anyone who comes in contact with this face over the next ten millennia is going to understand what's up with this site, that there's something about it that's dangerous, scary, and likely to make them sick. I like the idea of a design that just gives the viewer a 'mood,' but we're dealing with life and death here. The most responsible thing we can do in this case is give easily interpretable information. We're trying to help these people!"

What we know is that he probably left his house by five o'clock. Down the block on Pilestredet around the corner to the tram, or down the block on Pilestredet by foot to Karl Johan, he would have passed the place that's now a bar called

"Edvard's Bar and Grille," and then the all-day slices shop called "Edvard's Oven Fresh," and then a store across the street called "Scream If You Like Sweets!"

He could have cut through Grazing Place, where every citizen could keep cattle, and then walk across a bridge that linked the city to its shore.

But Edvard says he liked to walk—"I need to walk to think"—and knew a longer path up Ekeberg Hill and through its forest.

This was 1883, and it was very likely August.

Up the hill as Edvard walked he passed couples stretched on blankets, dozens of slanting bodies on the city's Lovers' Lane. Then he reached the forest once the meadow hillside leveled. And then he walked inside the woods, despite his father's warnings.

"There is evil there," his father said, "long forgotten curses from Norway's pagan past."

Edvard turned nineteen that year, and was living still at home. He would have needed his dad's permission to have been out past six thirty. He would have needed to miss his dinner, retired early to his room, established two days earlier that he was feeling kind of ill. He would have needed three years earlier to have had rheumatic fever, and needed twelve years earlier to have almost died on Christmas Day. And then he would have needed a low window he could climb through.

There was a gray straw hat he wore "every single day that I knew him, from the time that he was fifteen until he left home for Berlin," according to a memoir by Edvard's closest friend.

He would have needed that straw hat.

Some good walking shoes.

The light wool brown coat that all middle-class boys wore. He would have needed forty minutes to pass through Ekeberg's forest, and would have needed to understand its ancient pagan history, the 3,000-year-old practice of bringing infants there to die, digging narrow graves over which boulders were then laid so that the child didn't suffocate but rather starved to death—a practice that was so common by the early eleventh century that St. Olav, the Christian bishop who arrived to baptize pagans, wrote a letter to Norwegians enforcing three new Christian laws—

> "There shall be no more folk singing in God's northern kingdom, for these are not the sounds our Lord and Savior wants to hear . . .

> "There shall desist immediately all the eating of horsemeat . . .

> "And because all Christian lives begin with Holy Baptism, no longer may any child be left exposed if it's unwanted"

—the last of which proved so controversial for the pagans that one decade later, in the famous Gulathing's Law, a revision was applied in which "no healthy child may be exposed if it's unwanted . . . except if his toes are in the place of his knees, whose chin is turned around and connected to the shoulder, the neck upon his breast . . . the skin on his legs turning scaly in complexion . . . his two eyes on the sides of the poor child's head . . . or goat horns . . . a dog's tail. . . . The child must be brought to the forest, therefore, and buried where neither men nor cattle ever go," conditions which were apparently not uncommon at the time, for, as Jenny Jochens explains in *Women in Old Norse Society*, the low-valleyed villages and the high walls of mountains confined the majority of Norwegians to their homes, "forcing upon the culture a certain amount of inbreeding . . . and thus resulting in increasingly deformed infants at birth."

He would have needed to know the phrase "I christen thee at random, Jon or Johanna," the spell St. Olav wrote to ward off any *utburd*, the wide-eyed, pale, and hairless ghosts of Norway's exposed children—the thin hairless shrieking souls who haunted Ekeberg's forest, looking for their parents.

He would have needed to know that night, if one mistook him for its father, clinging to his back with a black and gaping jaw, that the only way to rid oneself at that point of an utburd is to convince the child to kill itself, and then bury it again.

But what he wouldn't have ever known, during his walk there as a teen, is that his childhood friend in fifteen years would kill himself in Ekeberg.

Wouldn't have ever known, once he had reached the other

side, looking down the hill to the city's ancient shore, that his sister would be committed, that he would never visit her, and that eventually she would die along the city's shoreline, through the forest, down the hill, in a loud and red asylum, from which the screams that were heard were so consistently high-pitched that local residents never forgot that it had been a slaughterhouse.

Wouldn't have ever known that this view he now walked toward would eventually be the city's most famous for postcards.

Most famous for drug arrests.

Most infamous for rape.

Wouldn't have ever seen, as he brushed off the forest leaves, the stone marker that the city will never place upon that spot, commemorating where Edvard first felt that he was hurt.

Won't see the bench that's there, the one turned the wrong direction.

Wouldn't need to cross the highway, where there is no crossing walk, approaching the metal guardrail, which no longer is a railing.

Wouldn't need to glimpse below to where the tracks are running now, to the service road, the power grid, the industry of concrete ports and forklift trucks and corrugated terminals for Unocal and Exxon and BP and Shell.

Didn't have to reach the bottom of that hill among the rocks.

Didn't need his parents dead, favorite sister, younger brother, older sister to be dead.

To help bleach their bloody sheets to light brown mottled spots with urine.

Didn't need to hate his father.

Love with fear his smiling mother.

Never needed to kiss a boy before he'd ever kissed a girl, and then to go on living without anyone to kiss.

Didn't need those critics saying that he'd invent something brand-new, that he would feel an ancient emptiness at the center of the world and then gather up that emptiness into something that had borders, a face, the chance to see what's wrong. Never needed someone saying that God is not in every detail, that God is sometimes in experience, someone to write letters to, from whom he could get letters back, take train trips with, and snuggle with, and then never to have met.

He didn't need the Earth, 10 million years ago, to rumble from the bottom of its ocean floor a mountain, a 4,000-acre island in Indonesia called Rakata, one of 13,000 islands in the narrow Sunda Strait on which the fabled Krakatoa, a mountain on the mountain—a volcano whose eruption in 1400 BCE is said to have caused tsunamis that were so big they sank Atlantis, a volcano whose eruption in 537 CE is said to have clouded skies so thoroughly that summer that it snowed in Rome in June, that crops in Europe failed, that floods appeared in deserts, that wandering Mongolians, retreating from the weather, fled with tribal families west into Eurasia, ended the Persian Empire, and started modern Islam—a volcano that locals called the "pulsing heart of all the world," never needed to erupt with so much power once again that on August 25, the week preceding Edvard's walk, it practiced an eruption at 5:30 in the evening, then practiced at 6:40, then 8:21, then 10:00, 10:50, midnight, and 1:00, and then finally at 3:30 on August 26, it erupted with a force that razed 160 villages, killed 40,000 people, burst so loudly that radiometrists have called the mountain's blast the second loudest noise ever heard by human beings, sending out concussive waves seven times around the world, and exploding up a mile high, and then exploding out: blanketing the atmosphere with 227 million tons of new debris, over two thirds of the island's entire rocky mass, dust that drifted across the Earth so thoroughly and fast that by August 28 British offices in Delhi were reporting having seen a bank of yellow clouds at night, by August 29 they were orange in Madrid, and by August 31 they mixed with moisture over London from where a cold front pushed the dust and rain westward over Norway, where the nights were very windy, and where light revealed that dust as red in skies that bled already.

His name was Levi Presley, the Vegas papers said.

Sixteen years old and from the north edge of town.

I tried to call his parents but their number wasn't listed.

I tried to go to his funeral but his service wasn't public.

I even called an ad that I had found in the yellow pages: *Venus Investigations.* A private investigation firm for "sensitive local cases."

Venus had a smoker's voice, a barking dog and screaming kids, and *Jeopardy* in the background.

Four hundred dollars cash, she said.

For "vital information."

I sent the money wired.

Five days later Venus called with Levi's middle name. She told me Levi's parents had first met in Arizona. She told me Levi hadn't ever committed any crimes. She told me where they lived, and then she said, "And there's a tape."

"A tape?" I asked.

"A security tape."

Every incident in a hotel in the city of Las Vegas is recorded by thousands of cameras that are embedded in the ceilings.

"So if someone's cheating at cards," Venus said over the phone, "or if there's a fight somewhere, a murder, any kind of shit, the hotel can edit together all the relevant footage and send it to the Vegas police. It limits their liability."

"And they made one of these of Levi?"

"That's what I'm hearing, man. Yeah."

"I wonder if I could see it."

"Now why the fuck would you want that?"

Levi liked going to Applebee's.

In-N-Out.

A place that's now out of business.

He wore a lot of white.

Sometimes a silver chain.

And purple-tinted glasses.

He liked a girl named Mary.

Also Eminem.

Was called by his mom "my little booper."

His Chrysler LeBaron was "Goose."

He said that he was sad.

I asked about what.

He said some stuff.

I asked like what.

Doesn't matter.

Why not.

Just sucks.

Hung up.

I sat beside the Presleys on a green leather La-Z-Boy sectional recliner with the ceramic black urn of Levi's ashes in my lap.

We were beneath their cathedral ceiling.

We were watching TV Land.

We had nuts and we had Triscuits and we had spinach dip and Coke.

We ate soup and then a salad and then chicken and then brownies.

We looked for several minutes at his art in their new den.

We drove across the valley to Tae Kwon Do for Kids, the studio Levi practiced at and coached others after school.

We sat in his coach's office among piles of trophy pieces.

We helped screw the golden kickers into braided sequined pillars and then dark wooden bases that read *ACHIEVEMENT* on their plaques.

We learned that Tae Kwon Do only has nine levels—there is white, yellow, orange, green, blue, purple, red, and brown, and then a whole series of advanced black belts, each with its own complexity of reticulated levels, nine tiers of nine grades in nine stages without end—because Korean culture does not believe we can be perfect.

We agreed this was significant because he fell for nine seconds.

I also learned that God resides in the ninth order of heaven.

That before he could receive the secret meaning of runes, Odin had to hang for nine days on a tree.

There are always nine Muses alive at any time.

Always nine maidens in ancient Celtic myths.

Always nine floors in sacred Buddhist temples.

If a servant finds nine peas in a pod and places that pod on the floor of her kitchen, the first man who comes in and tramples that pod will be the man she marries.

Possession, they say, is nine tenths of the law.

Nine people, says the Bible, will be stoned on Judgment Day.

Thrice to thine, and thrice to mine, and thrice again to make up nine is how Shakespeare's three witches guaranteed Macbeth's charm.

For nine, said Pythagoras, is that which brings completion.

I think we knew, however, that he really fell for eight.

Drove back to where they lived.

Made plans for dinner soon.

Kissed and hugged and waved goodbye and said we'd be in touch.

I left Las Vegas five months after Mom and I arrived.

At some point it came clear while I was visiting the Presleys that in fact I had not spoken to their son the night he died.

It was clear as I left Vegas that some other boy had called.

Clear that if I point to something seeming like significance, there is the possibility that nothing real is there.

Sometimes we misplace knowledge in pursuit of information.

Sometimes our wisdom, too, in pursuit of what's called knowledge.

WHY

Levi came home at 2:00 a.m., or he came home at 2:30 a.m. But neither Gail, his mom, nor Levi Senior, his dad, can remember exactly which. This doesn't matter, though, they both say, because his curfew was 11:00. "We didn't say anything immediately because he had a tournament the next day, and we knew he needed his sleep," Gail says. Levi slept for five hours or he slept for four and a half hours, then he woke, showered, dressed, ate nothing, drove to his tournament, stretched, cheered, competed, lost, drove back home, slammed the car door, slammed the front door, slammed his room door, and stayed there. "He was probably in there two hours," Gail says. Is that unusual? "That's not unusual," she says, "but after a tournament I guess it'd be a little unusual, because he really liked to talk about his meets when he came home." After another hour Gail says she and her husband called Levi into their bedroom and told him that he was grounded for staying out past his curfew and for being at a party to which, they suspected, other kids had brought drugs. Gail says she heard ecstasy. Levi Senior says pot. Levi said Fine, threw his cell phone on their bed, and told them that they might as well take that too. He slammed their bedroom door, slammed the front door, slammed his car door, and drove away. Is that unusual? "That's not unusual, he's a teenager," says Gail. "But then again we had just grounded him." Levi drove east down Pleasant Plains Way, turned right onto Rainy River, left onto Joe Michael, right onto Shermcreft, right onto Gowan, left onto Rainbow, right onto Cheyenne, south onto Interstate 15 past two exits, then right onto Sahara, left onto Vegas, left onto Baltimore, and right into the parking garage at the Stratosphere Hotel. He found a space on the fifth level, the blue level, three spaces away from the elevator. It was 5:18 p.m. Levi then either walked down two flights of stairs to the third level of the garage, the orange level of the garage, where a skywalk connects parking to the hotel's registration. Or Levi waited there in order to take the elevator. This was Saturday, however, and in the early evening hours on Saturdays in Vegas the elevators everywhere are slow. Once inside the casino, Levi walked down its red staircase and passed the Group Tours reception desk on his right side and Roxy's Diner on his left, where a disk jockey plays fifties rock and the waitstaff sings. Because it was a Saturday and early evening at Roxy's, "the place definitely would have been hopping," said their featured waiter, Johnny Pot Roast, who thinks he was on duty that night, he said. "And who knows, I was probably singing 'Greased Lightning,' 'cause it's a high-energy number and that's what we want on a Saturday night." When Johnny starts singing the waitresses pull microphones from the pouches of their aprons and jump onto the partitions between the diner's booths. They wave their order pads in the air and shimmy in place while diners lift forkfuls of potatoes to their mouths and Johnny jumps high and lands on his knees and holds his eyes shut as he holds the long *ing* in the long final high note in "lightning." Levi then walked past the casino's 48 card tables and 2,000 slot machines, some of which are named after popular American television shows   I DREAM OF JEANNIE, WHEEL OF FORTUNE, HOGAN'S HEROES— and some of which are named after popular American merchandise—SPAM, HARLEY-DAVIDSON, the board game BATTLESHIP—and some of which are not named after anything at all—MONEY TO BURN, THE NICKEL GAME, PUSH IT PUSH IT PUSH IT—and then Levi walked toward the woman at the foot of the escalator who sells cigarettes and cigars and battery-operated necklaces from a small tray that hangs from her shoulders below her breasts. There is a blue star necklace and a red orb necklace and a yellow cross necklace available for sale, each of which glows steadily or flickers randomly or even can be programmed "to reflect your own mood!" Amy, who was on duty that night, knows Levi didn't buy anything because she would have remembered a boy buying a necklace, she said. "Usually the guys who buy stuff are buying stuff for raves, and I always ask them where they're going 'cause I'm a raver, too." Then he went up the escalator. Levi would have stood in line at the hotel's ticket booth in order to buy a ticket to the top of the hotel's tower. Because it was Saturday and early evening, however, there would have been a long line at the hotel ticket booth. Levi would have stood between the fanny packs and the midriffs and the open containers and the flip-flops and noticed the backlit advertisements behind the hotel's ticket booth for the upcoming Billy Ray Cyrus concert in September or the Heavyweight Boxing Extravaganza in November or the Stratosphere's New Guaranteed Refund Slot Program, which pays players back 15 percent of what they've lost, and then he would have purchased his ticket from one of the three ticket booth attendants for four dollars rather than eight, because he was a Las Vegas resident, and finally he would have begun to walk toward the tower's elevator at the other end of the Stratosphere's Tower of Shops Mall. Past Flagmania. Past Alpaca Pete's. Past the Fabulous Las Vegas Magic Shop and the Great Wall of Magnets and Goldfather's, a kiosk that sells gold chains by the yard. Levi walked past Aqua Massage. Häagen-Dazs. Temporary Henna Airbrush Tattoo. Past Perfumania, Leather Land, Gifts Plus, Arcade. Past *COMING SOON TO THIS LOCATION ANOTHER EXCITING SHOP.* Past Stitch It On's hat embroidery kiosk. Past Vegas Candle's *HUGE BLOWOUT SALE!* Past Wetzel's Pretzels, Cleo's Fine Jewelers, and CJ's Casino Emporium,

which sells "vintage 1991" slot machines for $4,995. Levi
walked past Breathe, an oxygen bar, where you can "revive
your body, renew your spirit, relax your mind, and feel more
alive" for fifteen dollars per fifteen-minute dose, which
includes your choice of one of eighteen complimentary oxygen aromas, such as Nirvana, Watermelon, Clarity, Peach,
Sublime, Capuccino, Synergy, Dream, Chocolate, Eclipse,
Revitalize, or Tangerine. The girls at Breathe don't remember Levi stopping by the bar that evening, but they do recall
hearing about his jump once it occurred. "All I want to say,"
said Jenny, who manages the bar, "is that it's awful that it
happened, but I know for a fact that he wasn't on O_2 when
he did it." Then Levi reached the end of the mall and walked
down a ramp to wait in the next line. Because it was Saturday
and early evening, however, there would have been a long
line wrapping around the roped corrals four or five times and
stretching back into the mall. Harold, a security guard, eventually would have asked Levi if he had any metal in his pock-
ets, and, because he did, Levi would have emptied his car
keys into a white Stratosphere slot machine coin bucket,
walked through the metal detector, picked up his keys, and
walked into a narrow hallway to wait for the elevator to the
tower. Because it was Saturday and early evening, however,
the group with which Levi had waited in line would have
had to wait in that hallway even longer. It would have been
crowded and hot and yellow-lit that night, and for the long
meanwhile during which Levi waited he might have glanced
over the railing and seen below him the Stratosphere's amuse-

ment area that's called Strat-O-Fair, a passageway of carnival games beside the hotel's pool. There is the softball-throwing game called "Cat Splat" and the ring-throwing game called "Orb-a-Toss" and the ride-at-your-own-risk mechanical bull that's called "Vegas Cowboy": "Warning! This mechanical bull is designed to simulate the motion of a live bull. Therefore, there is a high probability that the rider will be thrown from, and/or struck by, this mechanical bull. This mechanical bull is a heavy duty machine that will violently, erratically, and unpredictably spin and rotate the rider at high speeds. You must be at least thirteen years old to ride this bull!" Then he entered the elevator. Inside, Levi would have been greeted by a young woman, perhaps Caroline, who would have worn black pants and a pink-and-teal Stratosphere polo shirt, and who would have announced, once the doors had closed, that Levi and the elevator's other twenty-five-maximum occupants that night would soon be traveling 1,858 feet per minute to the top of the Stratosphere tower, even though they would only be traveling 857 feet to the top of the Stratosphere tower, together, in a double-decker elevator in which they would have been so closely arranged that it would have been impossible for them to have counted themselves, some of whom might have been drunk, some of whom might have been talking over the elevator operator's narrative of their ascent, and some of whom might have interrupted the operator to ask her, several times, on the same trip, while giggling, how many times each day she goes up and down the shaft. Then Levi would have exited and walked into the blue-lit hallway of the first level of the tower's two-level observation deck, past a closed gift shop, past a closed snack bar, past the picture-paned radio station that had broadcast nothing for years, and into the carpeted round enclosure of the deck, whose floor-to-ceiling windows slant inward toward the ground so that visitors, while looking down at Las Vegas, toe-to-pane at the windows, might experience what pre-opening hotel press releases called, in 1994, "free-fall." Then he walked upstairs, outside. It was Saturday and early evening and there were many people around. Some kids running around the paved deck of the tower. Some adults looking through the coin-operated telescopes, making sure they wouldn't work before first depositing a coin. Some older people holding on to the inside chain-link fence of the deck, readjusting their grips each time a copter flew by. Levi walked left, east, away from where the sun had begun its own decline, and leaned briefly against the four-foot-high-railinged fence of the deck while a bride and groom took photographs of each other and then of the view and then of the last 200 feet of the tower above. Then Levi climbed over the four-foot-high-railinged fence, stepped into what Stratosphere security calls "the moat," a six-foot-wide concrete paved space between the four-foot-high fence on the deck's inside perimeter and the ten-foot-high fence at the very edge of the perimeter, and then Levi climbed over the ten-foot-high fence and sat down. It was Saturday and early evening and an alarm was ringing in the hotel's security office. Levi sat on the ledge for forty-eight seconds before anyone on the

deck walked by. Now the sun was gone. Saturday was night.
And the valley in which Levi had grown up became bright,
and it stayed bright, all the way to the invisible black mountains around it, the wall that would keep the city forever the
shape it now was. Security officer Frank then approached
Levi from the left, the east, and said, "Hey," or he said, "Hey,
kid," or he said, "Kid, no," or he said nothing, and it was his
presence alone that caused Levi to turn his head to the left,
stand up on the ledge, wave to the security officer, who does
not appear on the screen of the video on which Levi is wav-
ing, and jump.

ACKNOWLEDGMENTS

Grateful acknowledgment is made to those who appear in this essay, most especially Gail and Levi Presley, who generously welcomed me into their home to share their story about Levi. I'm grateful as well to Joshua Abbey, director of the Desert Space Foundation in Las Vegas, Nevada; to Vic Baker, Professor of Hydrology at the University of Arizona; to Lee Clarke, Professor of Sociology at Rutgers University; to Virginia Corning, Emeritus Professor of Climatology, Boulder City, Nevada; to Michael Brill, founding director of the Buffalo Organization for Social and Technological Innovation in Buffalo; to John Fildes, Medical Director of the Trauma Center at the University Medical Center in Las Vegas; to Ron Flud, former Coroner of Clark County, Nevada; to Robert Fri, Fellow at Resources for the Future in Washington, D.C.; to David Givens, director of the Center for Nonverbal Studies in Tacoma, Washington; to Bob Halstead, Transportation Adviser for the state of Nevada's Agency for Nuclear Projects; to Corbin Harney, Spiritual Leader of the Western Shoshone Indian Nation; to Sandra Harris, former director of the Las Vegas Neon Sign Association; to Dave Hickey, Professor of Art History at the University of Nevada at Las Vegas; to Michael Karnell, director of Otolaryngology at the University of Iowa; to Venus Lovetere, president of Venus Investigations; to Cory Martin, owner of Tae Kwon Do for Kids in Las Vegas; to Louis Narens, Professor of Cognitive Science at the University of California at Irvine; to Fritz Newmeyer, Professor of Linguistics at the University of Washington; and to Aaron Sell, Research Fellow at the Center for Evolutionary Psychology at the University of California at Santa Barbara. In addition, I'm grateful for the help of my friend Jon Wilcox, Professor of English at the University of Iowa, who provided me with the Old English translations that appear on page 128. And finally I am grateful to those other experts who spoke with me at length about the issues in this book, among them Allen Benson, director of Institutional Affairs at the Department of Energy in Las Vegas; Dorothy Bryant, former director of the Las Vegas Suicide Prevention Center; Gregg Ficke, founder of Vegas Action; Linda Flatt, chairwoman of the Nevada Coalition for Suicide Prevention; Frank Hoifodt, Research Fellow at the Munch Museet in Oslo, Norway; Maureen Kaplan, research analyst at the Eastern Research Group; Jerry King, project manager for Yucca Mountain's Feasibility Study at the Department of Energy in Las Vegas; Elise Lund, press liaison at the National Museum of Norway; Robert Lupton, former county liaison in the Office of Congressional and Intergovernmental Affairs at the U.S. Department of Energy; Lars Mehlum, director of Norway's National Center for Suicide Research and Prevention; Woody Sullivan, Professor of Astrobiology at the University of Washington; Steve Weeks, manager of the Young Electric Sign Company of Las Vegas; and Claire Whetsel, education specialist at the Yucca Mountain Science Center. I also want to thank the Lannan Foundation for a long and luxurious residency that helped kick-start this project. In addition I thank my friend Joanna Klink for having a better sense of what it was about than I did while trying to write it. I thank my editor, Jill Bialosky, for having endless faith in it. And as ever I thank my agent, Matt McGowan, for his endless faith in me. Finally, I am proud of my mother, Gaetana D'Agata, for not losing faith in Vegas.

NOTES

Although the narrative of this essay suggests that it takes place over a single summer, the span between my arrival in Las Vegas and my final departure was, in fact, much longer. I have conflated time in this way for dramatic effect only, but I have tried to indicate each instance of this below. At times, I have also changed subjects' names or combined a number of subjects into a single composite "character." Each example of this is noted.

Who

11   *If you take the population of Las Vegas, Nevada:* Most of the statistics in this essay are based on 2005 population studies.

12   *"You of all people":* The best source for details about the Las Vegas Centennial is the city's own centennial Web site, http://www. lasvegas2005.org/involved.

14   *"the happening of the century!"*: Antonio Planas, "Parade Recalls
      'Good Old Times,'" *Las Vegas Review-Journal*, May 15, 2005.

14   *"something special happened here!"*: David Mannweiler, "Las Vegas
      Celebrates 100 Years," *Indianapolis Star*, May 15, 2005.

14   if *"all that really happened?"*: Editorial, "Did All That Really Hap-
      pen?", *Las Vegas Review-Journal*, January 1, 2006.

14   *"as one of the greatest things"*: Quoted in *Las Vegas: An Unconven-
      tional History*, Public Broadcasting Service, *American Experience*,
      2005.

What

21   *"You gotta imagine the land out here"*: My mom went through a few
      real estate agents during that first summer in the city. "Ethan" is
      a composite of two of them.

21   *a lush haven that was named in 1829*: Las Vegas was named by
      Raphael Rivera, the first nonnative to explore the valley.

21   *"like a godsend"* . . . *"touched by God"*: Raphael Rivera is under-
      standably a mythic figure in Las Vegas. A bronze statue of the
      teenaged scout can be found beside the parking lot of the Raphael
      Rivera Community Center near downtown Las Vegas. I first
      heard about Rivera's discovery in 2004 while taking a walking
      tour of the city that was led by the Architecture Studies Library
      at the University of Nevada at Las Vegas. However, in recent
      years, historians have begun to doubt not only Rivera's stirring
      descriptions of those nineteenth-century meadows but also the
      discovery itself. In December 1829, Rivera was part of a trading
      party that was traveling from New Mexico to Southern Cali-
      fornia on horseback. On Christmas Day, the group reached the
      Virgin River, about 100 miles south of Las Vegas, at which point
      Rivera and an unnamed companion departed for what was called
      a "reconnaissance mission." Five days later, Rivera's companion

returned to the camp alone, without any knowledge of Rivera's whereabouts. After another seven days on his own, Rivera rode into camp on an exhausted horse, reporting only that he had found "a Mojave Indian village." And nothing else. According to a 2001 interview on KNPR with Frank Wright, curator of manuscripts at the Nevada State Museum and Historical Society, "none of the records that the trading party kept make any mention of Rivera describing a paradise of green meadows. . . . It was somewhat later, in fact, that an unknown party would happen upon the Las Vegas valley and record it on Mexican maps." (See Frank Wright, "Was Raphael Rivera the First European to Pass Through the Las Vegas Valley?" *Nevada Yesterdays*, KNPR, February 2001.)

22　*"the most successful master planned community"*: As Rosa Silver of the Office of Community and Government Relations, Howard Hughes Corporation, explained in a telephone interview on April 7, 2003.

22　*"Someone moves into a new Summerlin home"*: Confirmed by Melissa Warren in "Summerlin Embraces Its No. 1 Status with Group Hug Event," Howard Hughes Corporation press release, May 20, 2001.

24　*According to the Nevada Development Authority's annual brochure:* *Then and Now: Las Vegas Perspective 2005*, Nevada Development Authority, 2005, p. 9.

24　*the fastest growing metropolitan area in America:* Technically, this statistic refers to the state of Nevada's overall growth. However, the population of Clark County, which includes Las Vegas, constitutes 70 percent of the state's population, which makes any state statistic particularly applicable to both Clark County as well as Las Vegas. See Robert E. Parker, "The Social Costs of Rapid Urbanization," in *The Grit Beneath the Glitter: Tales from the Real Las Vegas*, ed. Hal K. Rothman and Mike Davis (Berkeley: University of California Press, 2002), p. 126.

24   *two new acres of land:* Launce Rake, "Las Vegas Sprawl Expands
      Ring Around Valley," *Las Vegas Sun*, September 5, 1999.

24   *an average of eight three-bedroom homes:* Hubble Smith, "Execs:
      Affordable Housing in Las Vegas Hinges on Planning," *Las Vegas
      Review-Journal*, February 13, 2003.

24   *the pipeline carries 97 percent:* Joe Schoenmann, "Low Water Mark,"
      Las Vegas Weekly, December 4, 2004.

24   *now ninety feet below what it normally:* Dana Wagner, "Dana Wag-
      ner's Drought Watch," KVBC News Las Vegas, November 15,
      2004.

24   *"58 percent of its usual capacity":* Stuart Leavenworth, "Parched
      Las Vegas: With Growth, Drought Both Relentless, the Desert
      Metropolis Faces a Crisis," *Sacramento Bee*, May 2, 2004.

24   *the lake will be completely dry:* Peter Weiss, "Lake Mead Could Be
      Dry by 2021," *Scripps News*, Scripps Institution of Oceanography,
      February 12, 2008.

24   *hydrologists from everywhere else:* See Joe Schoenmann, "Low Water
      Mark," *Las Vegas Weekly*, December 4, 2004, and Henry Brean,
      "Deepening Drought: Lake Level in Fast Fall," *Las Vegas Review-
      Journal*, June 18, 2004.

25   *"I'm not even sure":* Comment from Virginia Corning, emeritus
      professor of Climatology, Boulder City, Nevada, in e-mail cor-
      respondence during the fall of 2003.

25   *"the notion that we have":* Quoted by Launce Rake in "Water
      Official: Drought Won't Stop Growth," *Las Vegas Sun,* June 9,
      2004. It should be noted that in the years since my mom's move
      to Las Vegas, the neighborhood of Summerlin has attempted to
      reduce its water use by encouraging residents to replace their
      lawns with more regionally appropriate landscaping. Homeown-
      ers can receive a dollar for every square foot of lawn that they
      remove and replace with xeriscaping.

26   *a chimney stack from a concrete plant:* Scott Gold, "Drought Sends
      Flooded Towns to the Surface," *Los Angeles Times*, October 24,
      2004.

26 *the B-29 bomber:* George Knapp, "B-29 Found 54 Years After Crashing into Lake Mead," KLAS News Las Vegas, August 9, 2004.

27 *the sundae shop, etc.:* Reported in "Evaluating Underwater Sites," *Las Vegas Sun,* June 25, 2004.

27 *Even a 5,000-year-old city reemerged:* Telephone interview with the Lost City Museum in Overton, Nevada, one of Nevada's six state museums, which was established by the Civilian Conservation Corps when five miles of Pueblo Grande de Nevada, the "lost city's" actual name, were inundated by Lake Mead's waters in the early 1940s.

27 *it had come together in order to watch:* Excellent implosion coverage was provided by Dave Berns, "Abracadabra . . . Poof!", *Las Vegas Review-Journal,* April 28, 1998.

28 *that they needed to unseat the current record-holding huggers:* As estimated by Melissa Warren, "Summerlin Embraces Its No. 1 Status with Group Hug Event."

When

31 *"We are going to watch someone single-handedly":* A good example of the abundant faith Las Vegas once had in Senator Harry Reid can be found in Jon Christensen's "Can Nevada Bury Yucca Mountain?", *High Country News,* July 2, 2001.

32 *"What we are talking about today":* Senator Harry Reid presided over the Yucca Mountain debate on July 9, 2002, live on C-SPAN for approximately five hours.

32 *"Our Favorite Politician":* As reported in "Best of the Valley 2002," *Las Vegas City Life,* November 20, 2002.

32 *"The Most Powerful Man":* Scott Dickensheets, "The Power List," *Las Vegas Life* (October 2002).

32 *"Ever since I was elected to Congress":* See Senator Reid's official Senate Web site, http://reid.senate.gov/issues/yucca.cfm.

33   *that Americans would be less afraid:* Sara Ginsburg, *Nuclear Waste Disposal* (Laguna Hills, CA: Aegean Park Press, 1996), p. 27.

33   *the American Nuclear Energy Council began to lobby:* Ibid. p. 61.

33   *"Of course, there's no direct correlation":* The leader of my mom's local activist group met with me on several occasions during the summer of 2005 to discuss the Yucca Mountain project.

34   *To temporarily shift our attention away:* As was eventually revealed in a document by Kent Rorem and Ed Allison entitled "The Nevada Initiative: The Long Term Program," a confidential report submitted to the American Nuclear Energy Council in September 1991.

34   *Representative James Wright . . . convinced:* See Ginsburg, *Nuclear Waste Disposal*, p. 31.

34   *Representative Tom Foley:* Ibid.

34   *the state of Nevada . . . with the forty-fourth lowest:* "Population and Area," *U.S. Census 1980*, Bureau of the Census (Washington, DC: U.S. Department of Commerce, 1981).

35   *"There are one million people":* Quoted in Ginsburg, *Nuclear Waste Disposal*, p. 30.

35   *Senator James McClure:* Ibid., pp. 27–28.

35   *"I would like to meet the Senator":* Donald L. Barlett and James B. Steele, *Forevermore: Nuclear Waste in America* (New York: W. W. Norton, 1986), p. 129.

35   *Yucca Mountain would end up holding:* William L. Fox, "Mad Science: Bad Business Skewed Politics," *Las Vegas Life* (April 2001).

36   *Environmental Impact Statement:* This report was actually one of dozens of previous reports. My estimate of 65,000 pages is based on a page count of several of them, including the *Final Environmental Impact Statement for the Nevada Test Site and Off-Site Locations in the State of Nevada*, published by the Department of Energy in 1996; the *Draft Environmental Impact Statement for a Geological Repository for the Disposal of Spent Nuclear Fuel and High-Level*

Radioactive Waste at Yucca Mountain, Nye County, Nevada, published by the Department of Energy in 1999; and the *Supplement to the Draft Environmental Impact Statement for a Geological Repository for the Disposal of Spent Nuclear Fuel and High-Level Radioactive Waste at Yucca Mountain, Nye County, Nevada,* published by the Department of Energy in 2001, which themselves total over 9,000 pages.

36 *the senators started their debate:* The Senate debate on Yucca Mountain took place on July 9, 2002. All details concerning this debate come from observations I made based on C-SPAN's coverage.

41 *a 60 to 39 vote:* Steve Tetreault, "Yucca Mountain: Senate OKs Dump," *Las Vegas Review-Journal,* July 10, 2002.

41 *a result that had been predicted two weeks earlier:* See Vikki Kratz, "Yucca Mountain: Did Money Influence the Senate Vote?", *Open Secrets,* vol. 6, no. 57, July 10, 2002.

41 *soft money contributions had been distributed:* As reported in *Yucca Mountain: Nuclear Power Industry Contributions to Senators, 1997–2002,* Center for Responsive Politics, Washington, D.C., July 10, 2002. Similarly, Max Cleland from Georgia received $49,605, Ernest Hollings from South Carolina $47,750, Zell Miller from Georgia $28,500, Bill Nelson from Florida $27,350, Carl Levin from Michigan $21,749, Patty Murray from Washington $21,250, Richard Durbin from Illinois $21,050, Ben Nelson from Nebraska $5,450, John Edwards from North Carolina $1,000, and Patrick Leahy from Vermont $500. Herb Kohl from Wisconsin got nothing, but he voted for Yucca Mountain anyway.

42 *no explanation for the confluence that night:* I should clarify here that I am conflating the date of the Yucca debate and the suicide that occurred at the Stratosphere Hotel. In reality, these two events were separated by three days.

42 *a boy who jumped from the tower of the Stratosphere:* K. C. Howard, "Two Jump to Their Deaths at Separate Hotels," *Las Vegas Review-Journal,* July 16, 2002.

43   *voted to temporarily ban lap dancing:* "Lap Dancing," editorial, *Las Vegas Review-Journal*, July 14, 2002.

43   *When archeologists found:* Scott Sonner, "Hot Sauce Bottle Used in 1870 Found," *Las Vegas Review-Journal*, June 28, 2002.

43   *a game of tic-tac-toe:* Lisa Keim, "Oh Cluck," Tropicana Resort Public Relations Media Information, August 14, 2002.

43   *another suicide by gunshot:* Confirmed by Sheri Renaud, Clark County Coroner's Office, in e-mail correspondence, May 12, 2002.

43   *another suicide by hanging:* Ibid.

43   *caused a traffic jam:* Megan Foster, an eyewitness to the suicide, described this in an interview at the Aztec Inn, Las Vegas, Nevada, on September 27, 2002.

44   *Eventually I'd learn his name:* Most of the details of this boy's life come from interviews conducted with his parents during the summer and fall of 2002 at their home in Las Vegas, Nevada.

45   *Senator Harry Reid had accepted over $19,000:* As confirmed in *Yucca Mountain: Nuclear Power Industry Contributions to Senators, 1997–2002,* Center for Responsive Politics, Washington D.C., July 10, 2002.

45   *He'd taken $4,000 from Science Applications:* See Benjamin Grove, "Politicians Accepted Money from Yucca Mountain Contractors," *Las Vegas Sun*, April 19, 2000. Claiming that he was unaware of Science Applications's relationship to the Yucca Mountain project, Reid agreed to return this contribution.

45   *And he'd received $50,000 from Morrison-Knudsen:* Benjamin Grove, "Reid's PAC Took Donation from Yucca Subcontractor," *Las Vegas Sun*, October 26, 2000. Reid did not return this money.

45   *had received $2.5 million:* Chuck Neubauer and Richard T. Cooper, "The Senator's Sons," *Los Angeles Times*, June 23, 2003.

45   *the Western Shoshone Indians:* The full story of the Shoshone protest and their legal battle for Yucca Mountain was reported brilliantly

and thoroughly by Toby Eglund in "Yucca Mountain's Other Story," *The Gully*, March 28, 2002.

46 *"The said tribes agree":* The Ruby Valley Treaty is officially called the United States Treaty with the Western Shoshoni, 1863. It was ratified on June 26, 1866, and includes a total of 689 statutes.

46 *"I'm not a lawyer":* Further details about the Yucca Mountain controversy within the tribe were explained to me by Corbin Harney, Spiritual Leader of the Western Shoshone Indian Nation, in an interview at his home in Tecopa, California, on July 23, 2002.

48 *the United States Indian Land Claims Commission:* Keith Rogers, "Western Shoshones File Yucca Lawsuit," *Las Vegas Review-Journal*, March 5, 2005.

48 *"the final distribution of this fund":* Quoted in "Western Shoshone Payout Bill Clears Congress," www.indianz.com, June 25, 2004.

48 *the Western Shoshone Land Claims Distribution Bill:* Jerry Reynolds, "Bush Signs Western Shoshone Legislation," *Indian County Today*, July 9, 2004.

48 *a multi-billion-dollar mining corporation:* As confirmed in "Barrick Gold Corporation," *International Directory of Company Histories*, vol. 34 (Farmington Hills, MI: St. James Press, 2000).

48 *a major campaign contributor to Senator Harry Reid:* Thomas Edsall, "Balancing Nevada, National Interests," *The Washington Post*, February 1, 2005.

48 *the primary shareholder:* Lisa Wolf, "Shoshone Use Film, Courts to Fight Gold Mine on Sacred Land," *Environmental News Service*, December 3, 2007.

48 *the single most important source for domestically mined gold:* As reported in "Nuclear Waste, Gold, and Land Theft in Newe Sogobia," *Earth First*, vol. 24, no. 6 (2000).

Where

51   *I went to the Yucca Mountain Information Center:* At one point, there were several Yucca Mountain information centers throughout the state of Nevada. The center that I visited, in North Las Vegas, has recently closed. The only remaining one is in Pahrump, Nevada. The visit detailed here is based on several trips that I made to the center in the Village Meadows Mall between 2001 and 2003.

51   *"We are representing the city":* I have altered the identity of the teacher chaperoning these forty-five students, as well as the middle school they attended. The details of my interactions with this teacher and her students are a composite of experiences with two different Las Vegas public schools over a period of two years at the Information Center.

52   *an Educational Outreach Specialist named Blair:* The name and identity of "Blair" have been changed.

53   *School programs such as this:* See Ginsburg, *Nuclear Waste Disposal,* pp. 73–74.

53   *In fact, the Las Vegas superintendent:* Emily Richmond, "Garcia Seeking Bright Side of Yucca," *Las Vegas Sun,* November 7, 2003.

53   *Shelley Berkley introduced an amendment:* Steve Tetreault, "Berkley Calls on DOE to Fire Yucca Mountain Cartoon Character," *Las Vegas Review-Journal,* March 31, 2006.

54   *"I was pretty surprised therefore":* "Testimony of Dr. Victor Gilinsky, former member of the U.S. Nuclear Regulatory Commission," U.S. Senate Committee on Energy and Natural Resources, May 22, 2002.

55   *63,000 gallons of water:* William L. Fox, "Mad Science: Bad Business Skewed Politics," *Las Vegas Life* (April 2001).

55   *"it was apparent that the original standards":* Quoted by Matt Bivens in "The Yucca Lemon," *The Nation,* March 5, 2002.

56 *"a new kind of miracle metal"*: As revealed by Victor Gilinsky in "Miracle Metal an Embarrassment for Yucca Backers," *Las Vegas Review-Journal*, November 25, 2003.

56 *"We strongly urge you"*: Quoted by Ryan Slattery, "Independent Nuclear Dump Report: Waste Canisters Will Leak," *Indian Country Today*, November 12, 2003.

57 *But in a letter from the Department of Energy:* Ibid.

57 *So, on the morning of May 12:* See Suzanne Struglinski, "State Test Shows Corrosion at Yucca," *Las Vegas Sun*, May 12, 2004.

57 *"Don't you agree that your studies"*: Quoted in Matthew L. Wald, "Science Will Catch Up at Waste Site, U.S. Says," *New York Times*, January 31, 2002.

58 *a facility that was discovered:* As reported by Ginsburg in *Nuclear Waste Disposal*, p. 22.

58 *over 340,000 lethal doses:* Ibid., pp. 23–24.

58 *"Anything that we saw"*: Quoted in *The Bomb's Lethal Legacy*, Public Broadcasting Service, *Nova*, 1990.

59 *over 200 billion gallons of waste:* Ginsburg, *Nuclear Waste Disposal*, p. 23.

59 *"Let me be perfectly frank"*: Quoted by Doug J. Swanson in "Cost, Frustrations Soar as Nuclear Project Lags: Backers Admit Problems with Nevada Plan," *Dallas Morning News*, May 23, 1993.

59 *"vulnerable to waste"*: Ibid.

59 *"Maybe if we can find out"*: Quoted in "Environs: Environmental Notes," *Daily Camera*, August 2, 1993.

60 *the California Institute of Technology revealed:* Solveig Torvik, "Into the Rabbit Hole," *Seattle Post-Intelligencer*, April 21, 1998.

60 *running directly through Yucca Mountain:* See Ginsburg, *Nuclear Waste Disposal*, pp. 84–86.

60 *"massive upwelling"*: See James Flynn, et al., *One Hundred Centuries of Solitude: Redirecting America's High-Level Nuclear Waste Policy* (Boulder, CO: Westview Press, 1995), p. 23.

62 *About 10,000 years ago:* This history is relatively easy to track down, so I won't detail each of my sources.

62 *living side by side with werewolves:* This, however, might be harder to find. It was reported by David McKie in "Researchers Find Werewolf Fears 10,000 Years Ago," *Japan Times*, January 17, 2002.

63 *around the time the last dragons in Sweden disappeared:* This, too, is worth citation. There's a wonderfully absurd discussion about the origin of our dragon fantasies in Carl Sagan's *The Dragons of Eden: Speculations on the Origins of Human Intelligence* (New York: Ballantine Books, 1986), and then again (a little less absurdly) in David Jones's *An Instinct for Dragons*, (New York: Routledge, 2000). A report submitted to the British Royal Society in 1764 suggested that dragons died off in Europe in the ninth century.

63 *Atlantis was destroyed by a flood:* According to Plato in "Critias."

63 *it's when 45 percent of Americans believe:* As reported by Frank Newport in "Third of Americans Say Evidence Has Supported Darwin's Evolution Theory: Almost Half of Americans Believe God Created Humans 10,000 Years Ago," Gallup Poll News Service, November 19, 2004.

64 *The half-life of iodine-131: EPA Facts About Iodine*, Environmental Protection Agency, Washington, D.C., July 2002.

64 *still dangerous enough to kill someone:* See Rosalie Bertell, "Nuclear Radiation and Its Biological Effects," Center for Nuclear Responsibility, Washington, D.C., 2000.

65 *the Yucca Mountain Development Act of 2002:* Public Law 200 of the 107th Congress, which was House Joint Resolution 87, is actually only two sentences long. It passed on July 23, 2002.

65 *the Energy Policy Act of 1992:* Quoted in "Nevada Court Challenges the Selection of the Yucca Mountain Site," Nuclear Energy Institute, Washington, D.C., 2005.

66 *"Hi, sir":* My interview with Robert Fri took place by telephone on April 5, 2005.

67   *"The reason for imposing a time frame on the Yucca Mountain project"*:
      As reported by the Committee on Technical Bases for Yucca
      Mountain Standards in *Technical Bases for Standards at Yucca Moun-
      tain Standards*, National Research Council, Washington, D.C.,
      1995, pp. 55–72.

68   *"What we're dealing with here"*: Interview by telephone with Rob-
      ert Halstead, State of Nevada Agency for Nuclear Projects, March
      3, 2003.

68   *Seventy-seven thousand tons of spent nuclear waste:* "DOE Calls for
      Bigger Nuclear Waste Dump," Associated Press, December 9,
      2008.

69   *"Testing to Failure: Design of Full-Scale Fire and Impact Tests for
      Spent Fuel Shipping Casks"*: Delivered by Robert Halstead and
      Fred Dilger at the 32nd Annual Waste Management Symposium,
      February 29–March 4, 2004, Tucson, Arizona.

69   *the trucks carrying the nuclear waste:* As estimated by Robert Halstead
      and Fred Dilger in "How Many Did You Say? Historical and
      Projected Spent Nuclear Fuel Shipments in the United States,
      1964–2048," Waste Management Conference, February 23–27,
      2003, Las Vegas, Nevada.

70   *They'll arrive in Las Vegas:* This hypothetical highway accident is
      described by Matthew Lamb, Marvin Resnikoff, and Richard
      Moore in the report entitled *Worst Case Credible Nuclear Transpor-
      tation Accidents: Analysis for Urban and Rural Nevada* (New York:
      Radioactive Waste Management Associates, 2001). All details
      concerning this hypothetical accident have been taken from their
      report.

71   *rupturing approximately thirty minutes afterward:* J. L. Sprung, *Reex-
      amination of Spent Fuel Shipping Risk Estimates*, U.S. Nuclear Reg-
      ulatory Commission, 2000, quoted in *Hypothetical Baltimore Rail
      Tunnel Fire Involving Spent Nuclear Fuel* (New York: Radioactive
      Waste Management Associates, 2002).

73   *"a decontamination factor higher than 10"*: D. I. Chanin and

W. B. Murfin, *Site Restoration: Estimation of Attributable Costs from Plutonium-Dispersal Accidents*, Technadyne Engineering Consulting, Sandia National Laboratories, Carlsbad, New Mexico, May 1996.

74   *The study's evaluation:* As Bob Halstead explained in "Yucca Mountain Transportation Risk and Impact Issues," a presentation to the National Academies of Science Committee on Nuclear Waste Transportation, July 25, 2003.

75   *a figure of 1–in–27, 000 odds, thus making:* According to Michael Bluejay, the "Wizard of Odds," who estimates that one's chances of winning a $16 million Megabucks slot machine jackpot are 1 in 49,836,032. He also estimates that the chances of being kidnapped by radioactive monkeys which then attempt to convert you to Buddhism are approximately 1 in 46 million.

75   *"It's dangerous to concentrate so much":* My conversation with Lee Clarke took place by telephone on May 8, 2008. See also Lee Clarke, *Worst Cases: Terror and Catastrophe in the Popular Imagination* (Chicago: University of Chicago Press, 2006), pp. x–xi.

Why

83   *I drove with my mom and a friend:* My hiking trip with Joshua Abbey took place on July 15, 2002.

84   *Abbey often claimed on the jackets:* See James Cahalan, *Edward Abbey: A Life* (Tucson: University of Arizona, 2003), p. iii.

84   *"He liked the prophetic suggestion":* Ibid., p. iv.

85   *often left cars to their demise:* Ibid., p. 274.

86   *The Shoshone say that Yucca:* Interview at his home in Tecopa, California, with Corbin Harney, Spiritual Leader of the Western Shoshone Indian Nation, July 23, 2002.

86   *"Better a cruel truth":* Edward Abbey, *Abbey's Road* (New York: Plume, 1991).

86 *Originally, the plan in the U.S. was to recycle our nuclear waste:* Each of these plans is detailed by Ginsburg in *Nuclear Waste Disposal*, pp. 11–17.

87 *"We have a responsibility":* Helga Thue, "The Right to a Future," Sandia National Laboratories, Carlsbad, New Mexico, 1996, p. 3.

88 *"Why are we assuming":* See Gregory Benford, *Deep Time: How Humanity Communicates Across Millennia* (New York: Harper Perennial, 1999), p. 45.

89 *thirty-three times more than the United Nations' budget:* See "Proposed UN Budget for 2004–2005 to Reach $2.9 Billion, According to Outline Presented in Fifth Committee," 57th General Assembly, United Nations, September 12, 2002.

89 *"The problem that we're dealing with":* Peter C. Van Wyck, *Signs of Danger: Waste, Trauma, and Nuclear Threat* (Minneapolis: University of Minnesota Press, 2005), sections 12.3–14.5.

90 *"Planning a storage facility":* This letter from the Department of Energy is dated July 24, 1990. It is included in Kathleen M. Trauth, Stephen C. Hora, and Robert V. Guzowski, eds., *Expert Judgement Panel on Markers to Deter Inadvertent Human Intrusion into the Waste Isolation Pilot Plant*, Sandia National Laboratories, Livermore, California, 1993, p. B-3. It is important to note that this panel was originally formed to address the need to mark a site called the Waste Isolation Pilot Plant (WIPP), a salt cavern in Carlsbad, New Mexico, in which low-level nuclear waste material has already begun to be stored. Because this panel was the first of its kind in the world, the preliminary plans for Yucca's marker have subsequently relied heavily on the findings of this report.

92 *In his report to the Department of Energy:* Most of the details about Thomas Sebeok's proposal come from his report, *Communication Measures to Bridge Ten Millennia,* Office of Nuclear Waste Isolation, Battelle Memorial Institute, Columbus, Ohio, 1984.

92 *Sebeok believed that the universe is in fact composed of signs:* See Susan Petrilli, *Thomas Sebeok and the Signs of Life* (Cambridge, UK: Totem Books, 2001), p. 5.

93 *These days, there are 297 individual companies:* As a tour guide explained on an evening bus ride up the Las Vegas Strip, taken during the International Sign Association Exposition in Las Vegas, Nevada, on April 4, 2003.

94 *but even then their canvas sides were covered:* See Charles Barnard, *The Magic Sign: The Electric Art and Architecture of Las Vegas* (Cincinnati, OH: ST Publications, 1993), p. 63.

94 *the city's first professional sign-making store:* Ibid., p. 64.

94 *Today, just the base footings:* Ibid., p. 14.

95 *the executive director of the Las Vegas Neon Sign Association:* My tour of the Las Vegas "neon boneyard" with Sandra Harris took place on April 2, 2003.

96 *"All cities communicate some sort of message":* See Robert Venturi, Denise Scott Brown, and Steven Izenour, *Learning from Las Vegas* (Cambridge, MA: MIT Press, 1972), p. 4.

97 *"That's why I thought":* The opening of the Universal Warning Sign Design exhibition took place on February 1, 2002, at the Marjorie Barrick Museum on the campus of the University of Nevada at Las Vegas. All details concerning that show come from observations I made during the reception.

99 *"I wanted to leave my mark on Las Vegas":* Bob Stupak's efforts to build a new monument for Las Vegas are chronicled by John L. Smith in *No Limit: The Rise and Fall of Bob Stupak and Las Vegas' Stratosphere Tower* (Las Vegas, NV: Huntington Press, 1997), pp. 142–44.

100 *"Well, yeah":* My conversation with Dave Hickey took place in the Fireside Lounge at the Peppermill Restaurant in Las Vegas, Nevada, on December 15, 2002.

101 *In 1996, only two years after:* As reported by Ken McCall, "Tower Went Up Easier Than It Could Come Down," *Las Vegas Sun,* July 29, 1996.

102 *"Basically, you'd have to fell it":* Ibid.

103 *Initially, Bob Stupak wanted to build:* John Galtant, "Stupak Sets Sights on Steel Tower," *Las Vegas Review-Journal,* October 5, 1989.

103 *"But around that time my daughter":* Quoted by Smith in *No Limit: The Rise and Fall of Bob Stupak and Las Vegas' Stratosphere Tower,* p. 143.

104 *Since 1993, the Stratosphere Hotel has received:* See "Best of Las Vegas," *Las Vegas Review-Journal,* March 22, 1998, and "Best of Las Vegas," *Las Vegas Review-Journal,* January 13, 2002, as well as Smith's *No Limit: The Rise and Fall of Bob Stupak and Las Vegas' Stratosphere Tower,* p. xviii.

104 *There have also been eight fires:* A fire broke out during the tower's construction in 1993 ("Stupak Reaches Settlement in Lawsuit," *Las Vegas Sun,* Oct. 30, 1999); another one broke out during its opening celebration ("Smoke Strands Guests Atop Tower," *Las Vegas Sun,* May 1, 1996); another two months after that ("Stratosphere Fire," *Las Vegas Sun,* July 5, 1996); another a year later ("Wastebasket Fire Leads to Evacuation at Stratosphere," *Las Vegas Sun,* April 16, 1997); another ten days after that ("Smoke, But No Towering Inferno," *Las Vegas Sun,* April 26, 1996); another in 2000 ("Fire Sprinkler Suppresses Fire at Las Vegas Hotel and Casino," *Fire Engineering,* vol. 153, no. 3 [March 2000]); another three years after that ("Sprinklers Douse Stratosphere Fire," *Las Vegas Sun,* Jan. 13, 2003); and one two years following that (Mary Manning, "Traffic, Lake Deaths Mar Weekend," *Las Vegas Sun,* Sept. 6, 2005).

104 *one guest strangled to death:* As reported in "Two Arrested in Kentucky Man's Death," *Las Vegas Review-Journal,* June 1, 2000.

104 *a machine gun fired:* As reported in "Police Defend Coverage of Violence-Prone Area," *Las Vegas Sun,* March 12, 1997.

104 *a lawsuit involving:* John Wilen, "Stratosphere to Honor Stupak's Vacation Packages," *Las Vegas Sun,* April 6, 1998.

104   *the Federal Aviation Administration's warning:* Detailed by Smith in *No Limit: The Rise and Fall of Bob Stupak and Las Vegas' Stratosphere Tower,* p. 198.

105   *the response from the mayor of Las Vegas:* Cathy Scott, "Consultant Calls Tower Obstacle to Air Traffic," *Las Vegas Sun,* June 3, 1994.

105   *the rumor of an anomaly that locals called a "kink":* Smith, *No Limit: The Rise and Fall of Bob Stupak and Las Vegas' Stratosphere Tower,* pp. 163, 197.

105   *the hotel's stock price of $14 . . . its price of 2¢:* Gary Thompson, "Stratosphere Stock Mystery Explained," *Las Vegas Sun,* February 26, 1998.

105   *the $35 million . . . the $500 million:* Smith, *No Limit: The Rise and Fall of Bob Stupak and Las Vegas' Stratosphere Tower,* pp. 171, 214.

105   *the $800 million that it accumulated:* Brian Seals, "Stratosphere Creditors Coming Out of the Woodwork," *Las Vegas Sun,* May 1, 1998.

105   *the hotel's bankruptcy:* Adam Steinhauer, "Stratosphere Files Bankruptcy," *Las Vegas Review-Journal,* January 28, 1997.

105   *There was the man from Utah:* As reported by Joe Schoenmann, "Man Jumps from Stratosphere Tower," *Las Vegas Review-Journal,* January 7, 2000.

105   *The man from Britain:* "Man Jumps from Stratosphere Tower," *Las Vegas Review-Journal,* February 8, 2006.

105   *The jump by the producer:* "Heartbreak Hits 'Vegas Elvis' Reality Show," *Casino City Times,* April 13, 2005.

How

109   *The life span of black ink, etc.:* All of these details appear in Frank Kendig and Richard Hutton, *Life-Spans: Or, How Long Things Last* (New York: Holt, Rinehart & Winston, 1979), pp. 194–96.

109   *the laser-encrypted plastic:* See Benford, *Deep Time: How Humanity Communicates Across Millennia,* p. 61.

109   *A color photograph:* As estimated by Kendig and Hutton in *Life-Spans,* p. 200. See also pp. 189, 188, 198, and 91 for the details that follow.

110   *"It's the medium's fault":* My conversation with Vic Baker took place in his office at the Department of Hydrology on the campus of the University of Arizona, Tucson, Arizona, on November 21, 2005.

111   *In a report entitled* Durability of Marker Materials for Nuclear Waste Isolation Sites*:* Warren Berry's report, published by the Office of Nuclear Waste Isolation at the Battelle Memorial Institute in 1983, is quoted by Gregory Fehr, Thomas Flynn, and William Andrews in *Feasibility Assessment for Permanent Surface Marker Systems at Yucca Mountain* (Washington, DC: Department of Energy, 1996), p. 9.

112   *The society broadened its study:* Ibid., pp. 19–21.

113   *Synroc, on the other hand:* "Synroc," *Nuclear Issues Briefing Paper,* no. 21, Uranium Information Center, Melbourne, Australia, 2005.

113   *This is an idea that was first proposed:* See "A Review of Department of Energy's Radioactive High-Level Waste Cleanup Programs," Hearing Before the Subcommittee on Oversight and Investigations of the Committee on Energy and Commerce, House of Representatives, Washington, D.C., July 17, 2003.

114   *Defense spending in the United States increased by 60 percent:* Martin Calhoun, *U.S. Military Spending, 1945–1996,* Center for Defense Spending, Washington, D.C., July 9, 1996.

114   *"This is a project about faith":* My conversation with David Givens took place by telephone on August 27, 2002, and was supplemented by several e-mail exchanges about the panel's design process over the course of the following year.

116   *"But the best thing to rely on":* My conversation with Louis

Narens took place at his home in Del Mar, California, on July 24, 2002.

118 *According to administrators of the Thematic Apperception Test:* As detailed by Lon Geiser and Morris I. Stein, "An Overview of the Thematic Apperception Test," in *Evocative Images: The Thematic Apperception Test and the Art of Projection,* ed. Lon Geister and Morris I. Stein (Washington, DC: American Psychological Association, 1999), pp. 3–5.

119 *"The Thematic Apperception Test: A Paradise of Psychodynamics":* This report was written by Edwin S. Shneidman, and can be found in *Evocative Images: The Thematic Apperception Test and the Art of Projections,* eds. Lon Geiser and Morris Stein (Washington, DC: American Psychological Association, 1999), pp. 87–98.

121 *"probably the most profound psychological":* Ibid., p. 88.

121 *"Yeah . . . except languages have the unfortunate habit":* My interview with Fritz Newmeyer took place in the student union building at the University of Washington, Seattle, on August 26, 2002.

123 *Linguists estimate that there are currently 6,700 languages:* See David Nettle and Suzanne Romaine, "Where Have All the Languages Gone?," in *Vanishing Voices: The Extinction of the World's Languages* (New York: Oxford University Press, 2000), pp. 5–10.

124 *American linguist Morris Swadesh:* See Joel Sherzer's profile "Swadesh: From the First Yale School to Prehistory," in Morris Swadesh, *The Origin and Diversification of Language,* ed. Joel Sherzer (New York: Atherton Press, 1971).

125 *to construct a template of basic vocabulary:* As Swadesh explains in "The Progress of Babel," in ibid., pp. 213–26.

125 *He developed a list of 200 such words:* Ibid., p. 283.

126 *"If we can show by means of comparative linguistics":* Ibid., p. 224.

127 *"This is not a place of honor":* Quoted in Trauth, Hora, and Guzowski, eds., *Expert Judgement Panel on Markers to Deter Inad-*

vertent Human Intrusion into the Waste Isolation Pilot Plant, p. F123.

128   *"Nis weorðful stow":* This Old English translation of the panel's warning message was composed by Jon Wilcox, professor of English at the University of Iowa in Iowa City, Iowa.

128   *"This is not an honorable place":* This literal translation of the Old English warning message was also composed by Jon Wilcox.

Why

133   *It's estimated that only 40 percent:* Research findings in the field of suicidology are dramatically inconsistent. I catalogue these findings merely to make that point.

134   *Recently, Dr. John Fildes:* As reported by Christopher Hagen in "Suicide Watch," *Las Vegas Life* (April 1999).

135   *Sergeant Tirso Dominguez:* My conversation with the sergeant took place by telephone on September 27, 2002.

135   *" 'no comment' is not a productive response":* See *Reporting on Suicide: Recommendations for the Media and Public Officials*, Centers for Disease Control and Prevention, Atlanta, 1994.

135   *Eric Darensburg:* My conversation with Eric Darensburg took place by telephone on October 11, 2002.

135   *Bob Gerye:* I attempted twice to get a comment from Bob Gerye, once by telephone and once by fax.

135   *But it was Bob Gerye who did say:* As the mother of the boy I was investigating explained in an interview with me at the Olive Garden, Las Vegas, Nevada, on October 2, 2002.

136   *an eyewitness to that death:* I attempted to interview this witness in Las Vegas by telephone on September 26, 2002.

136   *Yet more people kill themselves in Las Vegas:* See Adam Goldman, "The Suicide Capital of America," Associated Press, February 9, 2004.

136   *you have a better chance of killing yourself:* Confirmed by Joleen
        Nemeth, Tim Pollard, Andrea Rivers, and Wei Yang in *Nevada
        Vital Statistics 2001–2003,* Nevada Department of Human
        Resources, 2005, pp. 201–03.

136   *one of the most dangerous places:* See David Littlejohn, "The Ulti-
        mate Company Town," in *The Real Las Vegas: Life Beyond the
        Strip,* ed. David Littlejohn (New York: Oxford University Press,
        1999), p. 7.

136   *more people kill themselves than die in car accidents, etc.:* Con-
        firmed by Nemeth, et al., *Nevada Vital Statistics 2001–2003,* pp.
        201–06.

136   *the highest number of smokers per capita:* See Parker, "The Social
        Costs of Rapid Urbanization," in *The Grit Beneath the Glitter:
        Tales from the Real Las Vegas,* ed. Rothman and Davis, p. 135.

136   *the highest rate of drug use among teenagers:* Marie Sanchez, "Growing
        Up in Las Vegas," in *The Real Las Vegas: Life Beyond the Strip,* ed.
        Littlejohn, p. 76.

136   *the highest number of American arrests:* Ibid., p. 85.

136   *The highest high school dropout rate:* Ibid., p. 7.

136   *Highest household bankruptcy rate:* Bob Lawless, "Bankruptcy Fil-
        ing Rates by District, April 2006–March 2008," at creditslips
        .org.

137   *the highest number of divorces:* See "America's Most (and Least)
        Stressful Cities," *Sperling's Best Places,* January 9, 2004.

137   *an average of 500 residents seek psychiatric treatment:* Larry Wills,
        "Mind Matters," *Las Vegas Mercury,* April 29, 2004.

137   *devotes just four . . . beds:* Damon Hodge, "Five Reasons Westcare
        Needs to Be Saved," *Las Vegas Weekly,* July 15, 2004.

137   *the homeless rate in Las Vegas quadrupled:* Quoted by Parker, "The
        Social Costs of Rapid Urbanization," in *The Grit Beneath the
        Glitter,* ed. Rothman and Davis, p. 141.

137   *dozens of downtown sweeps:* "Vegas Rated Nation's 'Meanest City'
        for Homeless," Associated Press, August 5, 2003.

137   *"The New All-American City," etc.*: As reported by Parker in "The Social Costs of Rapid Urbanization," p. 126.

138   *the single most stressful city*: See "Top Ten Most Depressed Cities," *Sperling's Best Places*, February 11, 2009.

138   *"The only real problem Las Vegas faces"*: Quoted in Hal Rothman, "The Many Faces of Las Vegas," in *The Grit Beneath the Glitter*, ed. Rothman and Davis, p. 14.

138   *"Another sign of how much America's"*: Sally Denton and Roger Morris, "Big Deal in Vegas," *Columbia Journalism Review*, vol. 39, no. 4, November 1, 2000.

139   *when Las Vegas casino owner Steve Wynn decided . . . and the story that follows*: Ibid. The publisher of John L. Smith's *Running Scared* was Barricade Books.

139   *provided several weeks' worth of coverage*: As reported by Michael Miner in "Rules of the Game," *Chicago Reader*, July 4, 2003.

140   *"With Jimmy Chagra on trial in Texas"*: Jim McManus, *Positively Fifth Street: Murderers, Cheetahs, and Binion's World Series of Poker* (New York: Farrar, Straus & Giroux, 2003), p. 44.

140   *"the Mayor took offense"*: Steve Sebelius, "Truth and the Media," *Las Vegas Review-Journal*, June 12, 2003.

140   *"Mayor Oscar Goodman may have defended"*: Michael Squires, "Full-page Apology to Goodman Appears in *New York Times*," *Las Vegas Review-Journal*, July 8, 2003.

140   *"ironies abound in Mayor Goodman's life"*: See John L. Smith, "Lack of Proof Linking Mayor to Murder Brings Swift End to Defamation Suit," *Las Vegas Review-Journal*, June 11, 2003.

141   *"not only was the allegation"*: John L. Smith, "Inaccuracies Don't Impair Sales of Book That Led to Goodman's Complaint," *Las Vegas Review-Journal*, June 13, 2003.

141   *a full-page ad appeared*: See Michael Squires, "'Outrageous Falsehood': Mayor Wins Retraction," *Las Vegas Review-Journal*, June 11, 2003.

141   *"We don't want anything in our city"*: Quoted in *Las Vegas: An Unconventional History*, Public Broadcasting Service, *American Experience*, 2005.

141   *the Nevada Motion Picture Division refused*: See Francisco Menendez, "Las Vegas of the Mind," in *The Grit Beneath the Glitter*, ed. Rothman and Davis, p. 47.

142   *"Well of course people are paranoid"*: As Ron Flud, Coroner of Clark County, Nevada, explained during two interviews on October 2, 2002, one of which took place over lunch at the Olive Garden, and another in his office later that afternoon. Ron Flud has since retired as Coroner of Clark County, Nevada.

143   *at the second Council of Orléans*: See Geo Stone, *Suicide and Attempted Suicide* (New York: Carroll & Graf, 1999), p. 16.

143   *The Talmud forbids even mourning*: C. W. Reines, "The Jewish Attitude Toward Suicide," *Judaism*, vol. 10, no. 2 (Spring 1961).

143   *Islam's ancient question*: See Leon E. Rosenberg, "Brainsick: A Physician's Journey to the Brink," *Cerebrum: The Dana Forum on Brain Science*, vol. 4, no. 4 (Fall 2002), pp. 43–60.

143   *Hindus condemn it*: Technically, a Hindu who commits suicide will go to neither heaven nor hell. Instead, he or she will remain in the earth's consciousness as a "bad spirit," wandering aimlessly until his or her allotted time has been fulfilled. So, suicide is not exactly condemned, but its repercussions are not a treat.

143   *the Buddha always forbade it*: There is, however, an argument that could be made that the Buddha would have allowed a suicide just as long as its victim had achieved enlightenment, as Michael Attwood explains in "Suicide as a Response to Suffering," *Western Buddhist Review*, vol. 4 (2005).

143   *there was an ordinance once*: Nils Retterstol, "Suicide in a Cultural History Perspective, Part 2," *Suicidologi*, 3 (2000).

143   *Psychologists were still debating the criminality*: See Edward Robb Ellis and George N. Allen, *Traitor Within* (Garden City, NY: Doubleday, 1961), p. 125.

145 *as Albert Heim . . . once did:* As Robert Owen reports in "The Near Death Experience," *British Journal of Psychiatry*, vol. 153 (1988), pp. 607–17.

146 *We were stopped at the southeastern guard gate:* I toured Yucca Mountain several times with different groups. The visit that is detailed here is a combination of those tours.

146 *the National Cancer Institute has subsequently determined:* See Miki Meek, "Compensating Life Downwind of Nevada," *National Geographic* (November 2002).

147 *During the nuclear testing that was conducted on the site:* Besides those details observed during my tours of Yucca Mountain, some additional details (including technical descriptions of the animals that were blown up at the site, the fabrics that were tested, and the housing structures that were studied) have been taken from Samuel Glasstone and Philip J. Dolan, *The Effects of Nuclear Weapons* (Washington, DC: U.S. Department of Defense, 1977), pp. 282–89.

148 *There is a bowling alley still on the grounds, etc.:* These details are reported in "Mercury, Nevada," *Nevada Test Site History*, National Nuclear Security Administration, Washington, D.C., 2005.

148 *A row of twenty newspaper vending machines:* Andy Walton, "Post-Nuclear Ghost Town: History Radiates from Artifacts at Nevada Test Site," *CNN Interactive*, 2005.

148 *one of America's seven National Nuclear Stockpiles:* See Keith Rogers, "Nuclear Bombs Stored at Nellis," *Las Vegas Review-Journal*, October 2, 1991.

148 *Fourteen hundred missiles await decommission:* As reported in "Half of U.S. Nuclear Arsenal in New Mexico, Georgia," CNN, August 26, 1997.

148 *"We have glorified gambling":* Quoted in *Las Vegas: An Unconventional History*, Public Broadcasting Service, *American Experience*, 2005.

149   *free twelve-month color calendars, etc.:* See Barbara Land and Myrick
      Land, *A Short History of Las Vegas* (Las Vegas: University of
      Nevada Press, 1999), p. 114.

149   *Miss Nevada praised:* "Miss Nevada, Newly Crowned, Supports
      Yucca Mountain," *Las Vegas Review-Journal,* January 20, 2006.

149   *250 people in the state of Nevada petitioned:* Ray Hagar, "Mushroom
      Cloud License Plate to Be Tested," *Reno Gazette-Journal,* April 23,
      2002. The proposed mushroom cloud license plate was eventually
      abandoned.

150   *God initiated this, etc.:* The predictions that follow come from a
      variety of sources, many of them dubious. The point here is only
      to illustrate their abundance.

151   *a study by the RAND Center:* Charles Meade and Roger Molan-
      der, *Considering the Effects of a Catastrophic Terrorist Attack,* RAND
      Center for Terrorism Risk Management Policy, Arlington, Vir-
      ginia, 2006.

152   *ten miles away from downtown Las Vegas:* Rogers, "Nuclear
      Bombs Stored at Nellis," *Las Vegas Review-Journal,* October 2,
      1991.

152   *the resulting blast would only take:* Estimated by Glasstone and Dolan
      in *The Effects of Nuclear Weapons,* pp. 24–31.

152   *if the temperature of the Sun is:* The temperature of the Sun's sur-
      face is actually 9,800° Fahrenheit, but the core is estimated to
      be around 15 million Kelvin, which is roughly 26,999,540° F.,
      according to Philip F. Schewe and Ben Stein, *The AIP Bulletin of
      Physics News,* 146, October 5, 1993.

152   *the temperature at which a human body combusts:* Depending on the
      weight of the body being burned, the Cremation Association of
      North America recommends that temperatures of crematoria be
      set at between 1400° and 2100° F. Approximately 95 percent of
      a human body will be vaporized at these temperatures.

152   *pain impulses in the human body:* The estimated speed of nerve
      impulses varies enormously for some reason—from as fast as 100

miles per second to as slow as a couple feet per hour—but the most reliable figure seems to come from David G. Myers, *Psychology*, 5th edn. (New York: Worth Publishers, 1998), p. 42.

152   *until sixteen hundredths of one second afterward:* Based on my own loose math.

153   *a man named Wally:* As noted earlier, I made several visits to Yucca Mountain, and I had a different guide for each trip. "Wally" is a composite of my more entertaining guides.

153   *"I've got you going with the press":* This portion of the tour is also a combination of several different trips, but each figure on the van represents an actual tourist who traveled with me.

158   *When I started to volunteer:* Details and quotations about this experience were gathered during a three-month period in the summer of 2002 when I volunteered as a counselor at the Las Vegas Suicide Prevention Center.

158   *Marjorie Westin:* I have changed the name and identity of the director of the center at the time I was volunteering.

158   *This is a variation on the standard:* Details about the Las Vegas Suicide Prevention Center's unorthodox procedures are reported very well by Stacy J. Willis in "Stopping Suicide: Nevada Lags Behind Nation in Prevention Programs," *Las Vegas Sun*, November 23, 2001.

159   *In comparison, the Suicide Crisis Call Line:* See Joan Whitley, "Calling for Help," *Las Vegas Review-Journal*, March 9, 2000.

160   *my mom and I attended a cake-cutting:* Details about the cake-cutting event are confirmed by Lisa Kim Bach in "Centennial Celebration Takes the Cake," *Las Vegas Review-Journal*, May 16, 2005.

160   *"All weekend people have been coming up":* Quoted in *Las Vegas: An Unconventional History*, Public Broadcasting Service, *American Experience*, 2005.

160   *It was seven layers high, etc.:* "Las Vegas Celebrates 100th Birthday with Giant Cake," *SIFY News*, May 16, 2006.

161   *organizers arranged to have it bulldozed:* As reported in "Swine Pig Out on Las Vegas' Birthday Cake," WNBC-5, May 17, 2005.

161   *after documents leaked by workers . . . showed proof:* Seth Borenstein, "Scientists Suspected of Falsifying Documents on Nuclear Waste Site," Knight Ridder, March 17, 2005.

162   *my mom moved out of Summerlin:* She now lives happily off Flamingo Avenue, a couple blocks from the Strip, in an unincorporated township called Paradise. The median income there is approximately $31,000, compared to about $78,000 in the community of Summerlin, which is eleven miles away from the Strip.

161   *a spate of suicides:* See Alan Maimon, "Experts Brace for Suicide Spike," *Las Vegas Review-Journal*, December 21, 2005.

161   *strange fish at Lake Mead:* As reported in "Water Contamination Affecting Fish," Associated Press, March 10, 2008.

161   *"the beginning of the extinction":* A fear that has been emphasized at length, and beautifully, by Timothy Egan in *Lasso the Wind: Away to the New West* (New York: Vintage Press, 1999), pp. 106–7.

163   *"I have often wondered why":* Quoted by Monica Bohm-Duchen in *The Private Life of a Masterpiece* (Berkeley: University of California Press, 2001), p. 172.`

163   *"I was walking along the road":* This is my own rough translation of one of Munch's many retellings of his experience with that sunset. It is based on a much more authoritative translation by Poul Erik Tojner, *Munch in His Own Words* (London: Prestel, 2003), p. 67.

164   *"I live with the dead every day":* Quoted in Bohm-Duchen, *The Private Life of a Masterpiece*, p. 153.

165   *It was there in Darwin too:* See Charles Darwin, in "Surprise, Astonishment, Fear, Horror," in *The Expression of the Emotions in Man and Animals*, ed. Francis Darwin (London: William Pickering, 1989), pp. 218–43.

167   *I think that what I believe is:* A few years after my first summer in
       Las Vegas, and nearly thirty years after the mountain's nomi-
       nation for waste storage, President Barack Obama—the fifth
       executive to oversee Yucca Mountain—vaguely indicated that
       he would like to "investigate the possibility of scaling back the
       Yucca Mountain project to some degree," a gesture to that 55
       percent of the state of Nevada that had helped him win the
       White House (cf. Marc Ambinder, "Eighteen States versus One
       Country," *Atlantic Monthly*, Sept. 17, 2008). Within a day of that
       announcement, Energy Secretary Steven Chu announced a plan
       to develop an "independent expert committee" to investigate
       the issue of nuclear waste storage—a committee, however, with
       rather limited independence, as it would also be "instructed to
       disregard Yucca Mountain as it performs its work" (Steve Tet-
       reault, "Yucca Missing from Plan to Remake Nuclear Waste
       Policy," *Las Vegas Review-Journal*, March 13, 2009). Not to be
       outdone, Senator Harry Reid announced one day later his own
       plan to form an "independent committee," one that he would
       instruct "to only consider 49 states in its review" (Steve Tet-
       reault, "Nuclear Industry to Fight Yucca Mountain Bill," *Las
       Vegas Review-Journal*, March 14, 2009). It goes without saying
       that the one excluded state in Harry Reid's plan would be his
       own home state of Nevada, which suggests, unsurprisingly, that
       none of this was about the science, not any of it about "what's
       right" or "what's fair," nor the "health and security of everyone
       in our state," nor certainly what Harry Reid had once referred
       to as "the honest truth."

Why

171   *"The reason why we scream":* My conversation with Aaron Sell took
       place by telephone on October 16, 2006.
173   *"We have equipment all over our bodies":* My conversation with

Michael Karnell took place in his lab on the campus of the University of Iowa, in Iowa City, Iowa, on October 18, 2006.

174   *"Even relatively simple changes can take tens":* Leda Cosmides and John Tooby, *The Adapted Mind: Evolutionary Psychology and the Generation of Culture* (New York: Oxford University Press, 1992), p. 21.

175   *only 39 percent of Americans believe:* As reported in a poll that was conducted by the University of Chicago in 1999 entitled *Reflections 2000.* The question was: "Will humans survive into the 22nd century?"

175   *There will also be a new axial tilt:* Martin Siegert, "The Day After Tomorrow," *The New Scientist,* vol. 184, no. 2476 (December 2004).

175   *lowering global temperatures by as much as:* As predicted by Alan Cooper and John Behrendt in *Antartica: The Dynamic Heart of It All,* Fact Sheet, U.S. Geological Survey, Washington, D.C., December 1, 2003.

175   *A new volcanic island will appear:* Predicted by Alex Tomimbang, "Hawaii's Land Grab, New Real Estate Everyday," *Hawaiicam,* June 28, 2004.

175   *And while we won't be living longer:* Predicted by Frank Tipler, *The Physics of Immortality: Modern Cosmology, God and the Resurrection of the Dead* (New York: Doubleday, 1994).

176   *Physicist John Fremlin believes:* See John Fremlin, "How Many People Can the World Support?", *The New Scientist,* vol. 24, no. 415 (October 1964).

176   *Rodney Brooks . . . believes however that humans:* Rodney Brooks, "The Merger of Flesh and Machines," in *The Next Fifty Years: Science in the First Half of the Twenty-first Century,* ed. John Brockman (New York: Vintage Books, 2002), p. 187.

176   *Warwick Collins:* This prediction was first posited by Collins in an essay entitled "Lock Up Your Laptops," *Prospect,* vol. 25 (December 1997). See also *Computer One* (London: Marian Boyars Publishers, 1997).

177   *we might look down at "Black Hole":* See Trauth, Hora, and

Guzowski, eds., *Expert Judgement on Markers to Deter Inadvertent Human Intrusion into the Waste Isolation Pilot Plant*, pp. F70–F71.

177   *Or we might stand on Yucca:* As described by Gregory Benford in *Deep Time: How Humanity Communicates Across Millennia*, p. 59.

177   *"pitch extraction from music":* Martin Braun, "Inferior Colliculus as Candidate for Pitch Extraction: Multiple Support from Statistics of Bilateral Spontaneous Otoacoustic Emissions," *Hearing Research*, vol. 145 (2000), pp. 130–40.

178   *Or we may see "Forbidding Blocks":* See Trauth, Hora, and Guzowski, eds., *Expert Judgement Panel on Markers to Deter Inadvertent Human Intrusion into the Waste Isolation Pilot Plant*, pp. F62–F74.

178   *But these will be environments:* As detailed by Michael Brill in "An Architecture of Peril," *Environmental and Architectural Phenomenology Newsletter*, Kansas State University (Fall 1993). Further details about the theories behind this part of the panel's recommendations were provided to me by Michael Brill, himself a member of the panel, and founding director of the Buffalo Organization for Social and Technological Innovation. Michael and I spoke by telephone during the summer of 2002. He passed away before we could meet in person in New York.

179   *a small series of twenty-foot-high monuments:* Gregory Fehr, Thomas Flynn, and William Andrews, *Feasibility Assessment for Permanent Surface Marker Systems at Yucca Mountain*, U.S. Department of Defense, Washington, D.C., 1996.

179   *"It's the most recognizable painting":* See, e.g., a report by Douglas Cruickshank, "How Do You Design a 'Keep Out!' Sign to Last 10,000 Years?", *Salon*, May 10, 2002.

179   *he probably left his house:* My walk along the route that Edvard Munch might have taken to see that sunset is speculative, of course. But there are guides all over Oslo who will volunteer to show you their own interpretations of Edvard's route to the shore. The most authoritative one is described by Frank Hoifodt in *Munch in Oslo* (Oslo: N. W. Damm & Son, 2002), pp. 12–15.

180   *"There is evil there":* Some of the more intimate details in this

walk are taken from Rolf E. Stenersen's memoir, *Edvard Munch: Close-Up of a Genius*, trans. Reidar Dittmann (Oslo: Gyldenal Norsk Forlag, 1944).

181 *needed to understand its ancient pagan history:* As Jenny Jochens outlines it in *Women in Old Norse Society* (Ithica, NY: Cornell University Press, 1995), p. 88.

181 *"There shall be no more folk singing":* Ibid., p. 90.

182 *"forcing upon the culture":* Ibid., p. 92.

182 *the wide-eyed, pale, and hairless ghosts:* The practice of child exposure in Norway was itself known as *utburd* (literally, "to set out"), which lent its name eventually to the ghosts that it produced. I learned about the superstitions surrounding *utburds* on a dog-sledding expedition I took outside Oslo during November 2002. We were actually looking for trolls.

183 *that his sister would be committed:* Bohm-Duchen, *The Private Life of a Masterpiece*, p. 153.

184 *He didn't need the Earth, 10 million years ago:* See Donald Olson, Russell Doescher, and Marilynn Olson, "When the Sky Ran Red," *Sky and Telescope* (February 2004).

185 *Venus had a smoker's voice:* My exchange with Venus Lovetere took place over a period of a few weeks during December 2002, by telephone, e-mail, and in person.

187 *I sat beside the Presleys:* I first met the Presleys together at their home in Las Vegas on October 2, 2002.

187 *We drove across the valley to Tae Kwon Do:* Levi's parents and I visited Tae Kwon Do for Kids on October 4, 2004. Levi's former coach, Cory Martin, taught us about the nine levels of belts in Tae Kwon Do.

188 *I also learned that God resides:* God does not reside in the ninth order of heaven, but at the time I thought He did. I misremembered Dante's claim that in the Ninth Sphere of Heaven, or the *Primum Mobile*, as he calls it, there is a "ring of happiness" in which all angels live, and at the center of which is a point of light

which Dante identifies as God. This is in *The Divine Comedy*, Canto 29.

188   *Odin had to hang for nine days:* According to the Old Norse poem "Hávamál" in the *Poetic Edda*, Odin hanged from what was called *Yggdrasill*, which translates literally as "Odin's horse," referring to the ancient idea of a gallows being the "horse of the hanged."

188   *There are always nine Muses alive:* According to the Greek poet Hesiod in his *Theogony*.

188   *Always nine maidens:* Nine maidens were often required in order to carry out important Celtic rituals, the most common of which were ceremonies involving cauldrons—the symbol of female strength—for which nine maidens were necessary to "keep a cauldron warm with a collective breath."

188   *Always nine floors:* Not *always*, but according to "The Development of Pagodas" in *The Beijing Review*, it is ideal that a pagoda have at least a nine-tiered steeple on its roof.

188   *If a servant finds nine peas:* Confirmed by Richard Webster in *The Encyclopaedia of Superstitions* (Woodbury, NJ: Llewellyn Publications, 2008), p. 182.

188   *Possession, they say:* See Mark Rose, "Nine-Tenths of the Law: English Copyright Debates and the Rhetoric of the Public Domain," *Law and Contemporary Problems*, vol. 66, no. 75 (2003), pp. 75–87.

188   *Nine people, says the Bible:* The Bible says a lot of things.

188   *For nine, said Pythagoras:* Pythagoras also considered nine "the finishing post," explaining that the number represents the conclusion of the series 1–9, and therefore "the last pure digit before the creation of hybrid forms." In *A Beginner's Guide to Constructing the Universe: The Mathematical Archetypes of Nature, Art, and Science*, Michael Schneider amplifies Pythagoras's philosophy by calling nine "the horizon that lies at the edge of the shore before the boundless ocean of numbers that repeat in endless cycles. . . . Nine is thus the unsurpassable limit, the utmost boundary, the ultimate

extension to which the archetypal principles of number can read and still manifest themselves in the world" (p. 302).

188 *I think we knew, however, that he really fell:* This is confirmed by the Clark County Coroner's "Report of Investigation, Case Number 02–04648," which details that Levi was observed by video surveillance jumping from the Stratosphere's observation deck on the 109th floor at 5:58:34 p.m. "According to security cameras," the report explains, "it took 8 seconds for the decedent to reach the pavement at 5:58:42 p.m., 833 feet below."

189 *Sometimes we misplace knowledge . . . Sometimes our wisdom, too:* These two lines are loosely adapted from a pageant play that T. S. Eliot wrote in 1934 entitled *The Rock*. It was performed as a fund-raiser for Anglican churches in London. The exact lines are: "Where is the wisdom we have lost in knowledge? / Where is the knowledge we have lost in information?"—Choruses, Part I, "The Rock," in *The Complete Poems and Plays of T. S. Eliot* (London & Boston: Faber & Faber, 1969). Our word "wisdom" comes from the Indo-European root *wid-*, which means "to see." "A wise man has no extensive knowledge," Lao-tzu once wrote. "He who has extensive knowledge is not a wise man."

Why

193 *Levi came home at 2:00 a.m., etc.:* The details of Levi's last few hours come from a variety of sources, including his parents, his Tae Kwon Do coach, some vendors in the mall at the Stratosphere Hotel, and my own observations while retracing his steps. These details were all accurate in 2002, the year that Levi died, but I know that some of them are now out of date. Several of the stores, kiosks, and restaurants described here have since moved to other locations or gone completely out of business. But I have chosen to be loyal to the facts and images that surrounded Levi as he made his way to the tower on that summer evening.